Intersections:
Where Faith and Life Meet

A Cumberland Presbyterian
Adult Resource
Volume 14, Giving

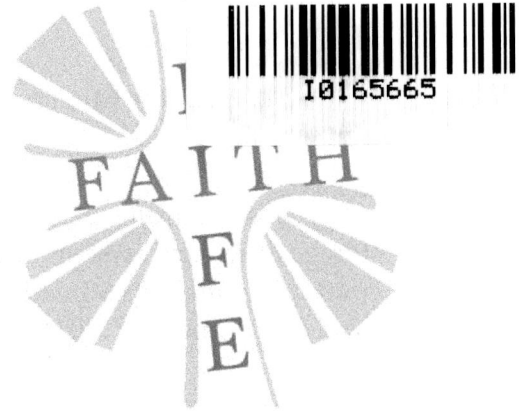

Discipleship Ministry Team
Ministry Council
Cumberland Presbyterian Church

8207 Traditional Place
Cordova, Tennessee 38016

First Edition 2016

Published by The Discipleship Ministry Team
General Assembly Ministry Council of the Cumberland Presbyterian Church
Cordova, Tennessee

ISBN-13: 978-0692482995
ISBN-10: 0692482997

We want to hear from you.
Please send your comments about this curriculum to
the Discipleship Ministry Team at chm@cumberland.org.

OUR UNITED OUTREACH
Made Possible In Part By Your Tithe To Our United Outreach

Table of Contents

Editor: Cindy Martin
Proofreader: Pam Campbell

To order, call 901-276-4572, x 252 or e-mail resources@cumberland.org.

God's Gift of Creation

Scripture for lesson: Genesis 1:26–2:1-3, 15-17; Psalm 8:3-8

American Presbyterian minister Patricia Tull recalls being on a train from Nepal to India with her daughter when a nun boarded and sat opposite them. The nun was wearing the white and blue associated with Mother Teresa's Missionaries of Charity. She describes being entranced by the woman, caught up in the romanticism about Mother Teresa and the order of the nuns.

As the train sped through the countryside, Tull was captivated by the beauty of the mountains of South Asia—a part of the world she had never before seen. Moved by the beauty of the creation and the sense that she was encountering a holy moment, she shared her joy through a smile to her daughter and then to the nun, who was eating her lunch.

Tull had been eating a banana and was wondering whether or not it would be proper to throw the skin from the train. Just then the nun stood up, packed her plastic knife, fork, cup, and napkin into a neat little box of trash; walked over to window; and tossed the entire package out the window. She then sat down and took out a prayer book.

Prep for the Journey

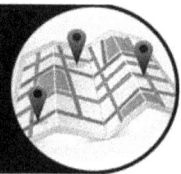

Genesis is a book of beginnings. With the call of Abraham in chapter 12, we have the beginning of what will become God's people, the Israelites. Before we get there, we have chapters 1-11, which biblical scholars consider to be primeval history. Although the entire book of Genesis is an ancient text, these early chapters seem to be some of the oldest stories known to human civilization. They are not the only stories from the ancient world. In fact, the accounts in these chapters —including the creation and flood stories—bear many similarities to stories from other cultures. The biblical record is not the only account of how the world came to be, but it does contain the particular stories

---

What strikes you about this story? How does the story demonstrate the various ways that we view the earth and our role in it? How are prayer and care for the creation spiritual? Explain your answer.

told by those who came to be known as Israel. Their stories reveal the particular ways in which they understood God, themselves, and the world.

As Christians, we follow in the tradition of faith that looks to Genesis for our beginnings. We look to these stories that have been told throughout the history of God's people for an understanding of God, ourselves, and our world. At the beginning of our journey into the exploration of giving, we turn to Genesis as we remind ourselves of our story, of who and whose we are, from where we come, and why.

On the Road

Our story begins with God. One of the most basic confessions of Christianity, and of all Abrahamic faiths, is that God alone is the Creator of all things, both human and non-human. God called all creation into being, gave it order, and sustains it. All of creation is totally dependent on God.

Read Genesis 1:26-27.

Then God said, "Let us make humankind in our image, according to our likeness; and let them have dominion over the fish of the sea, and over the birds of the air, and over the cattle, and over all the wild animals of the earth, and over every creeping thing that creeps upon the earth."

[27] So God created humankind in his image,
*   in the image of God he created them;*
*   male and female he created them.*

God's plan included giving humans great responsibility for all that was created. We are to care for the earth as God intended: to share it for the good of all.

Read Genesis 1:28-31.

God blessed them, and God said to them, "Be fruitful and multiply, and fill the earth and subdue it; and have dominion over the fish of the sea and over the birds of the air and over every living thing that moves upon the earth." [29] God said, "See, I have given you every plant yielding seed that is upon the face of all the earth, and every tree with seed in its fruit; you shall have them for food. [30] And to every beast of the earth, and to every bird of the air, and to everything that creeps on the earth, everything that has the breath of life, I have given every green plant for food." And it was so. [31] God saw everything that he had made, and in-deed, it was very good. And there was evening and there was morning, the sixth day.

When have you tried to take control of your life rather than being dependent on God? What caused you to recognize that you had to rely upon God?

Other than with gratitude, how do people respond to life and the creation? How can humankind treat the physical—living things, the sea, and the soil—as holy creations of God? How can we treat the spiritual—our souls—as holy creations of God?

The words *subdue* and *dominion* are misleading because of their aggressive associations, but biblical scholars say that these words should be understood as care-giving and nurturing. Unfortunately, in many instances humans have failed to be the caretakers God intended and have destroyed many parts of God's creation.

In the words of Patricia Tull, "gratitude is a most appropriate response for us as inhabitants of this world, a home we neither bought nor paid for nor could have ever designed." Just take a quick glimpse through the psalms and you'll find this kind of attitude in the prayers and songs of the psalmists who repeatedly praise God for the beauty of the creation and the gift of life. Our faith story begins with God giving.

Scenic Route

Reread Genesis 1:26-27.

Then God said, "Let us make humankind in our image, according to our likeness; and let them have dominion over the fish of the sea, and over the birds of the air, and over the cattle, and over all the wild animals of the earth, and over every creeping thing that creeps upon the earth."
²⁷ So God created humankind in his image,
in the image of God he created them;
male and female he created them.

Something unique happened when God created humans. With every other part of creation, God simply said, "Let there be," and there was. But when it came to humans, God's speech changed to, "Let *us* make humankind in *our* image, according to *our* likeness."

Why does this matter? By consulting with others, God shared the creative power. As humans, we are created in the image of a God who creates by sharing power with others.

To whom do you think God was speaking? Why do you think the creative process suddenly became a consultation?

Read Psalm 8:3-8.

When I look at your heavens, the work of your fingers,
the moon and the stars that you have established;
⁴ what are human beings that you are mindful of them,
mortals that you care for them?

⁵ Yet you have made them a little lower than God,
and crowned them with glory and honor.
⁶ You have given them dominion over the works of your hands;
you have put all things under their feet,
⁷ all sheep and oxen,
and also the beasts of the field,

8 the birds of the air, and the fish of the sea,
whatever passes along the paths of the seas.

The very origins of the world show God's generosity to creation. God not only created, but God provided (and continues to provide) for creation. The delicate balance of nature and the way the food chain works is amazing. God had a purpose for creating every living creature, even mosquitoes!

Life is a gift to all of creation, and humans have been invited into a unique partnership with God to be in continual giving to the earth. Notice that God does not simply put humans in charge of what has already been finished. Creation is an ongoing work with land that needs to be tilled, crops that need to be harvested, ecosystems that need to be protected, and new life to be produced.

Read Genesis 2:15-17.

The LORD God took the man and put him in the garden of Eden to till it and keep it. 16 And the LORD God commanded the man, "You may freely eat of every tree of the garden; 17 but of the tree of the knowledge of good and evil you shall not eat, for in the day that you eat of it you shall die."

God provided bountifully for creation, giving an ample and renewable supply of everything that creation needed to flourish. God gave only one restriction to humankind: "Of the tree of the knowledge of good and evil you shall not eat." Humans were to till the garden and keep it. They were free to eat of its bounty, but not to destroy it. These verses give some insight into what God meant by giving dominion.

The creation in Genesis 1 is not a static paradise where humans are given the place of honor to consume and exploit to their hearts content, but a productive world in which they are called to accept the invitation to be partners with God, taking up the responsibility to care for all of God's creation.

Workers Ahead

From the beginning, God called creation "good"; when it was complete, it was very good—all of it. The human and the non-human, the physical as well as the spiritual, the body as well as the spirit, the soil as well as the soul. God says, "See, I have given you…" (verse 29). It is good, and it is a gift.

If we stop reading at the end of chapter 1, we would only have made it to the end of the sixth day. We need to read the rest of the story.

What similarities do you find between the passage from Psalm 8 and the creation story from Genesis? Why do you think the psalmist may have written these words?

What are your thoughts about being in a partnership with God? Why? How are you involved in the ongoing work of creation?

Why is it that we always seem to want what isn't best for us? When have you experienced the consequences of choosing something that wasn't in your best interest? How did that experience affect your life?

What kind of imagery or metaphor might describe the role of humans that Genesis 1 envisions?

Read Genesis 2:1-3.

Thus the heavens and the earth were finished, and all their multitude. ² And on the seventh day God finished the work that he had done, and he rested on the seventh day from all the work that he had done. ³ So God blessed the seventh day and hallowed it, because on it God rested from all the work that he had done in creation.

Perhaps if we weren't so familiar with Genesis 1, we might be able to sense God's delight in the creative process more fully. Six times throughout the creative process God declared that it was "good." At the end of the sixth day, "God saw everything that he had made, and indeed, it was very good" (verse 31).

We have a tendency to think of humans as the pinnacle of creation because we were the final work of the process. But if we read carefully, we find that humans share the sixth day with the creation of all other living creatures.

Sabbath rest, on the other hand, gets an entire day on of its own. Sabbath is more than just a neat bow on the creation, more than an accommodation for finite or lazy humans. Sabbath is at the heart of God and the Christian story. The pinnacle of the creation is God's restful and delighting presence.

We are called into partnership with God, to join in the creative action in the world, but just as God is not a workaholic, neither should we be. The concept of sabbath is an invitation simply to be, to remember that it is all a gift, and that it is good. There is a time to work, a time to play, and a time to rest. Rest is difficult in a culture of frantic activity and consumption. Practicing sabbath requires us to accept that life is a gift to us, not a right or an obligation. Sabbath requires us to resist the temptation to believe that we are the primary characters in the story; it calls us to remember that we are God's, that we inhabit God's good creation.

How do you observe the sabbath? When have you experienced rest as spiritual? What regular practices of sabbath rest do you have? How might you adapt them to be more spiritual?

In the Rear View

The story of the nun from the beginning of the lesson revealed an attitude that is puzzling to many—an attitude that views prayer as something spiritual, but does not consider care for creation as being in relationship with God. The Christian story doesn't make such a separation. It's all holy, it's all a gift, and God invites us to participate in the ongoing creative work of stewardship. We are recipients of a gift and called to live in the image of the Gift Giver, the One who shares power for the good of all creation.

Travel Log

Day 1:

Psalm 104 is a song of thanksgiving that recalls God's creative work in nature. Find somewhere that you are comfortable reading Psalm 104 aloud. If possible, do so outdoors. If any verses particularly resonate with you, write them in your own words in the space below.

Day 2:

Make a list of things for which you are grateful. Offer a prayer of thanksgiving to God.

Day 3:

Take a walk today, paying particular attention to the world around you. What elements of nature did you notice? Whom did you see? What did you notice that you had not noticed before? Make some notes below.

Day 4:

God invites us to share power for the good of all creation. Make a list of how we have misused that power in ways that are destructive for the world. Write the words *forgive us, Lord* after each item on the list.

Day 5:

Make a list of ways you can give to creation. You might plant flowers that are especially welcoming to butterflies, use "green" cleaning products, recycle, use an alternate source of energy, etc. Take your list and get started!

Day 6:

We are created in the image of a God who creates by sharing power with others. What kind of power do you have over creation? How do you use it?

Choose a word that describes the kind of power you have as a steward of God's creation and then write about it. What might God be inviting or challenging you to do?

Day 7:

Sabbath is the practice of ceasing all work to enjoy the creation and the Creator. Make two columns in the space below. In one column, list the ways in which you can practice sabbath. In the other column, list the things that block you from practicing sabbath.

Sources

Inhabiting Eden: Christians, the Bible, and the Ecological Crisis, by Patricia Tull. Louisville: Westminster John Knox. 2013.

The Curse of Resentment

Scripture for lesson: Genesis 4:1-16

In the opening scenes of Disney Pixar's classic *Toy Story*, a child named Andy is happily playing with his toys. We learn that the toys, which come to life when Andy leaves, care deeply for one another and for Andy. But when a new toy, a space ranger by the name of Buzz Lightyear, shows up, everything changes. When Woody the Sheriff, one of Andy's favorite toys, sees Buzz, his eyes widen and his jaw drops. Not only is Buzz shiny, new, and high-tech, but worst of all, he's in Woody's spot.

Buzz explains that his ship must have crash landed in the room by mistake. "Yes, it is a mistake," Woody replies. "You see the bed here is my spot." In these simple words are the seeds of what will grow into a deep and divisive resentment. When the gift of being Andy's toys and the joy of their beloved community becomes a right, which is focused on self, there are implications not just for Woody and Buzz, but for all the toys and their owner.

Prep for the Journey

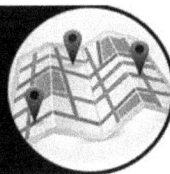

The humans God created lived in the paradise of the garden of Eden for a while, but after sinning against God, they had to leave. Scripture tells us that God sent them from the garden to till the ground. In other words, they had to work for what God had previously given them in the garden. We also learn that Eve gave birth to two sons: Cain and Abel.

Read Genesis 4:1-2.
Now the man knew his wife Eve, and she conceived and bore Cain, saying, "I have produced a man with the help of the LORD." ² Next she bore his brother Abel. Now Abel was a keeper of sheep, and Cain a tiller of the ground.

In what other examples, real or fictional, have you noticed resentment impacting relationships? When have you felt threatened by someone's presence? How did you respond?

How might you have felt about having to work for what had previously been freely provided?

How has the web of relationships been abused in your life? How can you restore this web?

It is possible that Genesis 3 and 4 were originally independent stories, coming from different traditions, but were edited together. Both stories reflect the struggle to live faithfully in God's world on God's terms. Adam and Eve's rebellion was primarily against God, while Cain's was against his brother. The first story reveals the difficulty of maintaining vertical relationships between God and humans. The second one exposes the strife of horizontal relationships between humans. Together they reveal how God, humans, and the earth are bound together in a web of interconnected relationships. When these relationships are abused, God's gift of life becomes a curse.

On the Road

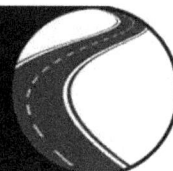

The story of Cain and Abel has remarkable similarities with that of Adam and Eve. 1) It begins with things as they should be; 2) a conflict emerges; 3) an act contrary to the divine will is committed; 4) the perpetrator is interrogated by God; 5) the perpetrator offers a defense; and 6) the perpetrator is expelled.

Read Genesis 4:3-5a.

In the course of time Cain brought to the Lord an offering of the fruit of the ground, 4 and Abel for his part brought of the firstlings of his flock, their fat portions. And the Lord had regard for Abel and his offering, 5 but for Cain and his offering he had no regard.

How do you see yourself as continuing in God's creative work?

Despite the rebellion of Adam and Eve in chapter 3, Cain and Abel's story is set in a scene of stability. Eve's proclamation that she had produced a man with the help of the Lord was a reflection of thanksgiving that she had been able to continue in God's creative work. The name *Cain* comes from the Hebrew word "to create."

The story begins with humans doing what they had been invited to do. Cain is a farmer, tilling the ground; Abel is a shepherd, tending to the livestock. We have a vision, if only for a moment, that all is well. They are engaged in partnership with God in continuing the creative and nurturing work of God in the world. Despite the disobedience of Adam and Eve in Genesis 3, there seems to be the continued possibility of people living faithfully in the world. In Abel's name, however, is a clue to the evil that lurks around the corner. In contrast to Cain's name, which reflects productivity and possibility, *Abel* means futile or empty.

What might have caused Cain and Abel to bring offerings to God?

Cain and Abel, farmer and shepherd, both bring an offering to God. This image of offering crops and livestock is common in the Old Testament, so we aren't likely to notice that Cain and Abel have not been instructed to make an offering. Later this kind of ritual offering will be explained and formalized in the life of God's people, but Genesis simply assumes that this is how God's creation responds to God: with gratitude and worship. Both brothers engage in this act of worship, but God only has regard for one. Both give gifts, but only one is received.

Our assumption is that God had a reason to reject Cain's gift. We find it hard to believe that God would just arbitrarily reject one person's worship over another, especially siblings. But nothing in the text suggests that there was anything inherently right or wrong about Cain's gift. There is no evidence of rivalry or ulterior motives. There seems to be no reason for God's lack of regard for Cain's gift; scripture does not provide an explanation. Those who are looking for some teaching about what makes worship or giving righteous won't find it here.

So what do we find in the story? Renowned Old Testament scholar Walter Brueggemann says that Cain's experience reflects what we all come to realize naturally: Life is unfair. Life is full of disruptions, conflict, and stress—particularly in a family. In addition, the God who is the source of our hope doesn't always act as we expect. Nor does right worship necessarily result in God's favor. While we don't find any evidence that Cain's offering was in some way less righteous than Abel's, his response does raise questions about our attitude toward worship.

Read Genesis 4:5b-8.

But for Cain and his offering he had no regard. So Cain was very angry, and his countenance fell. ⁶ The LORD said to Cain, "Why are you angry, and why has your countenance fallen? ⁷ If you do well, will you not be accepted? And if you do not do well, sin is lurking at the door; its desire is for you, but you must master it."

⁸ Cain said to his brother Abel, "Let us go out to the field." And when they were in the field, Cain rose up against his brother Abel, and killed him.

The rejection of Cain is confusing and joins a long tradition of scripture that leaves us without an answer. The tension in Cain's story is how he will choose to respond to what he perceives as the unfairness of life, and even of God. In verse 7 God responds to Cain's anger, pointing out the choice that he faces.

After reading Adam and Eve's story in Genesis 3, we might imagine that sin has already so infected humanity that all people are inevitably drawn toward it. But chapter 4 is actually the first mention of the word *sin* (4:7). Walter Brueggemann points out that sin is not described as doing a wrong act, but as a force that compels and lures, similar to the serpent in chapter 3. The word *lurking* evokes the image of a predator ready to consume and devour Cain. But God is clear that Cain has a choice and that he possesses the capacity to master anything that lures him away from right a relationship with God and his brother.

Why do you worship God? When has it been difficult for you, your family, or your congregation to worship God? What was that experience like?

How do you feel about the lack of explanation regarding God's rejection of Cain's offering? How might you have reacted in that situation?

Where do you see situations that are unfair? How do those situations make you feel? How do you deal with that anger?

What does this story tell us about the nature and path of resentment and anger? Why do you think Cain reacted so strongly against Abel?

How do you feel about Brueggemann's description of sin? When have felt as if sin was devouring you? a friend? the world?

What constitutes a healthy relationship with our Creator? How have your actions damaged your relationship with God? with others?

In what instances are you guilty of shifting the blame? How do you feel when someone shifts the blame to you?

How difficult is it for you to accept the responsibility for and consequences of your actions?

When Adam and Eve acted against God's will, their relationship with God was damaged. Cain's act damaged his relationship with another human, specifically his own brother. It also damaged his relationship with God because he had taken an innocent life. Although Abel had done no wrong, his life ended in futility at the hands of his brother's rage.

Many of us need no reminder of how fragile family relationships can be and how unresolved conflict can result in great pain. Many people have experienced sibling rivalry—the intense competition, the complex and often conflicting emotions of having brothers and sisters. This story evokes for us an awareness of the danger that anger and resentment can cause within families and all relationships. We know all too well that sin is lurking at the doors of our relationships, desiring to consume us with resentment and an anger that divides.

Scenic Route

It always seems easier to shift the blame to someone else rather than accept the consequences of our actions. Apparently humans have always had this tendency.

Read Genesis 4:9-16.

Then the LORD said to Cain, "Where is your brother Abel?" He said, "I do not know; am I my brother's keeper?" [10] And the LORD said, "What have you done? Listen; your brother's blood is crying out to me from the ground! [11] And now you are cursed from the ground, which has opened its mouth to receive your brother's blood from your hand. [12] When you till the ground, it will no longer yield to you its strength; you will be a fugitive and a wanderer on the earth." [13] Cain said to the Lord, "My punishment is greater than I can bear! [14] Today you have driven me away from the soil, and I shall be hidden from your face; I shall be a fugitive and a wanderer on the earth, and anyone who meets me may kill me." [15] Then the LORD said to him, "Not so! Whoever kills Cain will suffer a sevenfold vengeance." And the LORD put a mark on Cain, so that no one who came upon him would kill him. [16] Then Cain went away from the presence of the LORD, and settled in the land of Nod, east of Eden.

When Adam and Eve heard God walking in the garden, they were afraid and hid. Adam blamed Eve, who in turn blamed the serpent. Cain responded that it was not his job to watch over his brother. If anyone is the keeper, it ought to be God. The lack of willingness to take responsibility for their actions is clearer in Cain's story than in Adam and Eve's, as is the severity of the consequences. Genesis 4

16

may mirror chapter 3 in many ways, but it also portrays an escalation in humanity's capacity for destruction.

Cain's resentment and the murder of his brother clearly result in the death of his human relationships, but it also has consequences for the earth, which will withhold its power from him. Not only does this add stress to his labor, but Cain sees being driven from the soil as "being hidden from [God's] face" (4:14). In Genesis 1 we see that God, humanity, and all of creation are bound together in a web of interconnectedness. In Genesis 4 we see the consequences for these damaged relationships. Brothers are estranged, lives are ended, humans become estranged from the goodness and fruitfulness of creation, and God is hidden.

And yet…verse 15 is clear: God does not let go, even of the one who has been consumed by sin, whose hands are red with guilt. The mark of Cain acts both as a sign of guilt, but also of protection.

Workers Ahead   CAUTION

God was unmistakably clear with Cain. He had a choice, and the stakes were high. The same is true today. Violence is increasing throughout the world, often claiming the lives of innocent bystanders. We can either learn to channel our anger into positive channels or more people will die.

When violence is rampant, we may wonder where God is, if God has hidden God's face from us. As God responded to Cain, the blood of those who have died is crying out to God, and it should be crying out to us as well. God has given us this world and placed us in the position of caregivers for all creation, which includes other people. God gave life and we are to treat it as being very good.

If we do not act to stop the violence that is destroying creation, we are failing in our responsibility to God. Only when we stop responding to anger with anger, violence with violence, will it stop. Anger and violence continue to provide fuel for the fire; love and acceptance will extinguish it. Only by working in partnership with God can peace be achieved.

What signs of broken relationships in the web of God, humanity, and creation do you see today? What does the story as a whole tell us about humanity? What does the story as a whole tell us about who God is?

How can you work for peace? How can your group/congregation work for peace? What are you actually willing to do to achieve peace? Where should you start?

In the Rear View

How will you respond to God for the gift of life to yourself and to all creation?

God made a "very good" creation, but by giving humans the ability to make choices, sin entered the world. People are drawn to the lure of sin, just as Eve was drawn to the serpent. It is the church's responsibility to help strengthen people's faith so that they will turn away from sin.

Cain's journey started out as an act of worship. When God rejected Cain's offering, Cain became angry and resentful. If these emotions are not mastered, they are frequently expressed through acts of violence. What started out as an act of gratitude for God's gift of life and provision became a self-centered expression of what Cain thought God owed him.

Sin is lurking at our door, just as it was at Cain's. Its desire is for us, but we must master it.

Travel Log

Day 1:

Psalm 6 is a prayer of petition, asking for God's presence and mercy in the midst of pain. It is the type of prayer that Cain might have prayed after being banished from his homeland. Take your Bible and go to a place where you are comfortable reading this psalm aloud as a prayer of confession. If you particularly connect with any words, write them in the space below. Try writing some of the verses in your own words. What do your reflections tell you?

Day 2:

"Sin is lurking at the door; its desire is for you, but you must master it." Draw a picture of a door frame, and inside it write behaviors or thoughts that threaten your relationship with God, the world, or others.

Day 3:

The problem is not Cain's anger with God, but that he let it consume him and surface in destructive ways. What are some destructive ways that your anger, resentment, and frustration surface? How can you channel that anger into something positive?

Day 4:

Recall a time when you felt angry at God. Write to God about that time, sharing honestly without fearing judgment. What happened? What did you feel toward God? What did you want to ask or say?

Day 5:

Make a list of relationships that are important to you. List at least one way that you can show appreciation for each relationship this week.

Day 6:

Cain and Abel's story reflects how the gift of life can become a curse once we become disconnected from our relationships to God, the creation, and others. What things that should be gifts have you come to take for granted? What gift has become a curse in your life? Why? What do you need to do in order to appreciate it as a gift?

Day 7:

What are some practical steps you can take to maintain or establish your relationships with God, the creation, and others? List those steps below.

Source

Genesis: in Bible Commentary for Teaching and Preaching, by Walter Brueggeman. Atlanta: John Knox Press. 1982.

Take, Go, and Offer: Divine Disorder

Scripture for lesson: Genesis 22:1-14

Mike King is the founder of Youthfront, a contemplative youth ministry camp in the town of LaCygne, Kansas, which is south of Kansas City. He tells the story of Carrie, a college graduate who came to work at the camp for a summer before settling into a high-paying new career with a large international corporation. The girls in her cabin adored her, and she found great energy from mentoring them. By the third week, she began to discuss with Mike the possibility of changing her plans and going into youth ministry. As the summer went by, doubts about her corporate career began to escalate, as did her sense of call to youth ministry. Aware of how camp can foster "mountaintop" experiences, Mike affirmed her gifts for ministry, but urged her not to make any decisions based on an emotional high.

Later in the summer, Mike received a call from Carrie's parents. They explained that even though they were active members in their church, they were concerned about Carrie's pursuit of youth ministry. "Carrie has just finished college and prepared for this wonderful job opportunity that will enable her to support herself and begin an exciting career. How will she support herself doing youth ministry? We think she's overreacting, and we want you to discourage her from doing this."

Reflecting on the conversation, Mike asks, "Do we really want our kids to follow the call of God on their lives?" Do we really want to follow the call of God? Reflecting on Carrie's experience, his own, as well as the endless challenging stories of the Bible, Mike concludes, "Following God is not safe."

The story of Abraham and the binding of Isaac is a story that raises questions about the cost of God's call, the expectations of God, and the risks of faith.

What experiences similar to either Carrie or her parents have you had? What is your reaction to the statement, "Following God is not safe"? Why do you feel this way?

Prep for the Journey

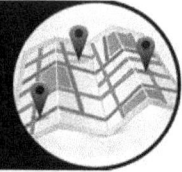

The introduction of Abraham at the end of chapter 11 marks a shift in Genesis from primeval to ancestral history. While Abraham's story is a continuation of the ancient stories of creation, chaos, and restoration, it is also the dawning of a new era in Genesis. This time was the beginning of an age in which God covenanted with a particular people, promising that through them would be a future for all humanity.

The ancestral history begins with God's words to Abraham, "Go from your country and your kindred and your father's house to the land that I will show you." God promised to establish a great nation through Abraham and Sarah, one that would bless the world. However, Abraham and Sarah were elderly and did not have a male heir.

No male heir meant that there was no future, no legacy, no blessing, and certainly no great nation. This new era of God's promise for humanity seemed to be over before it began, yet God did not relent. Though Abraham attained fatherhood through the birth of a son to Sarah's maid, Hagar, Ishmael was not the son God had promised. The birth of Isaac in chapter 21 marked the fulfillment of God's promise, but it also resulted in the casting out of Ishmael, an event that caused Abraham great distress (21:11).

However, the promise was called into question when God told Abraham to make a difficult and disturbing gift. We now turn to one of the most well-known and most challenging stories in our scriptures.

On the Road

God's command to Abraham in Genesis 22:1 is similar to the one made at the beginning of chapter 12. God's original call required Abraham to forsake his past, leaving his home and family for a destination unknown to him. Now God's call requires him to go to another unknown destination, this time to forsake his future.

Read Genesis 22:1-3.

After these things God tested Abraham. He said to him, "Abraham!" And he said, "Here I am." [2] He said, "Take your son, your only son Isaac, whom you love, and go to the land of Moriah, and offer him there as a burnt offering on one of the mountains that I shall show you." [3] So Abra-

How might you have felt/ reacted in Abraham's sandals?

When have you struggled to believe God's promise? Why?

How do the lesson comments put Abraham's story in a different perspective?

ham rose early in the morning, saddled his donkey, and took two of his young men with him, and his son Isaac; he cut the wood for the burnt offering, and set out and went to the place in the distance that God had shown him.*

Having already suffered the pain of sending Ishmael away in chapter 21, Abraham faced the prospect of losing another son. So, why might Abraham have accepted that God would demand he offer his son as a sacrifice?

At this time, most people worshiped multiple gods and practiced human sacrifice as a way of showing their faith. Thus, it is understandable why Abraham apparently did not question God's command. After all, shouldn't Abraham have been willing to exhibit the same level of faith as those who worshiped false gods?

We know what Abraham did not—that God was testing him. Despite the obvious contradictions of God's promise of a child and the command to sacrifice him, Abraham responded with silent obedience. The text gives us no clue as to Abraham's emotion, leaving us to imagine what he may have been thinking.

We have no way of knowing how old Isaac was at this time. Some scholars speculate that he may have been a young man; it is doubtful that he was still a small child because he understood enough about the purpose of the trip to question why they had not brought a lamb for the sacrifice; he also carried the wood that they would use.

Read Genesis 22:4-8.

On the third day Abraham looked up and saw the place far away. ⁵ Then Abraham said to his young men, "Stay here with the donkey; the boy and I will go over there; we will worship, and then we will come back to you." ⁶ Abraham took the wood of the burnt offering and laid it on his son Isaac, and he himself carried the fire and the knife. So the two of them walked on together. ⁷ Isaac said to his father Abraham, "Father!" And he said, "Here I am, my son." He said, "The fire and the wood are here, but where is the lamb for a burnt offering?" ⁸ Abraham said, "God himself will provide the lamb for a burnt offering, my son." So the two of them walked on together.

When Isaac called to him, Abraham responded in the same way he had responded to God in verse 1, saying, "Here I am." His response reflects that he was fully present to his son, as he was to God, standing in an agonizing tension of loyalty and love to both.

Abraham was not just blindly and unthinkingly obedient to God's commands, but he trusted God to provide another way. Believing that God would provide was, nevertheless, a risk. We should not assume that Abraham's trust of God was easy. Instead, it may be more honest and helpful to appreciate the complexity and anguish of a faith in the One who is beyond our control and whose actions we cannot always comprehend.

Faith is not uncritical or unthinking acceptance of the divine, and Abraham demonstrated both holy obedience and holy resistance.

How do you feel about God testing Abraham? How has God tested you? What helped you to face the test?

What might Isaac have been experiencing as they made this trip? When have you had to accept something on faith?

In what ways do you identify with Abraham's experience of faith? When have you resisted what God was telling you to do? Why? What makes your religion real to you?

"Abraham was not blessed for correctness in conception of God's will; he was blessed because when he thought he knew God's will he was willing to obey it to the limit (*The Interpreter's Bible, Vol. 1*, © 1952, page 645). Only when we are willing to obey in such an all-out fashion is our religion truly real.

Scenic Route

Read Genesis 22:9-14.

When they came to the place that God had shown him, Abraham built an altar there and laid the wood in order. He bound his son Isaac, and laid him on the altar, on top of the wood. [10] Then Abraham reached out his hand and took the knife to kill his son. [11] But the angel of the Lord called to him from heaven, and said, "Abraham, Abraham!" And he said, "Here I am." [12] He said, "Do not lay your hand on the boy or do anything to him; for now I know that you fear God, since you have not withheld your son, your only son, from me." [13] And Abraham looked up and saw a ram, caught in a thicket by its horns. Abraham went and took the ram and offered it up as a burnt offering instead of his son. [14] So Abraham called that place "The LORD will provide"; as it is said to this day, "On the mount of the LORD it shall be provided."

In his book *Counterfeit Gods*, Presbyterian minister Timothy Keller says that human hearts are idol-making factories that turn good gifts from God into things of ultimate worth. He describes an idol as "anything so central and essential to your life that, should you lose it, your life would feel hardly worth living." These things can be physical objects, social relationships, social status, and even hopes or beliefs. Abraham, he says, is being tested on where his ultimate allegiance lies. Is it with the Creator of the gift, or the gift itself? Is it his son, or the One from whom that son came? Abraham passed the test and Isaac was spared at the last minute. Abraham was prepared to give up that which was most valuable in an act of worship to the God who gave it to him.

God did not, however, require the sacrifice of Isaac. The issue was not Isaac himself, but the value that Abraham assigned to him. If Abraham was to be the one through whom God would establish a covenant with humanity, an assurance of faithfulness was necessary. God required Abraham's undivided loyalty, evidence that he was willing to stay the course—even in the face of the impossible. If such loyalty is the prerequisite for selection to God's call, we can imagine how many nominees may have failed before God found one who would stay the course.

What kinds of things order your life and give it value? How might these things be a gift but also a curse in the journey of faith?

To whom or what do you give undivided loyalty? What evidence to you have that your loyalty is justified?

Workers Ahead

In the ancient world, the inability to have children was not only a denial of a deep and personal longing, but it was also considered to be a sign of a divine curse. In that culture, a male heir was not just someone to take care of property, but a source of honor and blessing. Abraham and Sarah had neither. Because their peers would have assumed that they had done something to deserve childlessness, they would have endured public shame and humiliation. The gift of a child, a male, restored their dignity and their honor.

Infertility in the modern world is a painful reality for many women and men who desire to bear their own children. Listening carefully to their experiences can surely shed light on the dark pain Sarah and Abraham experienced.

The church can be one of the most uncomfortable and unwelcoming places for people who do not have children. So many activities are focused around the "typical" family, which includes children, that those who do not have children often feel excluded. Think about those times when a family is asked to light the Advent candle and only those who have children are invited to participate, or when we sit in family groups at a potluck meal and fail to include others. The church should be the one place where people feel welcomed unconditionally.

Whom do you know who is struggling with infertility? How can you be supportive of them during this time?

In what ways may your congregation be making people feel uncomfortable or unwelcome? How can you change those attitudes?

In the Rear View

The Christian story begins with God bringing order to chaos, but God's continued presence in human life often produces the opposite result: it is chaos to our order. A calling to be God's people means a reordering of our lives around God, which results in inevitable conflict and confrontation with the order we have created. An unavoidable challenge of this reorientation is our relationship to that which is most valuable to us.

When God's people hold too tightly to the gifts of God and to the world as they have ordered it, they forsake their call. They become too focused on maintaining the world as they desire it, as it makes them feel safe, as it makes sense to them, protecting what is theirs. Inevitably, they become focused on their world and those who belong in it, marginalizing those who challenge or threaten it. The gifts of God become a curse and a weapon.

What will give us ultimate meaning and guidance in our lives? What are the good gifts of God that have given ultimate value?

What questions or challenges does this text raise for you? What does it reveal about God, and about us? What would your response to God have been?

The calling of God requires an openness to holy disturbance and the disordering of our lives that we may be found in God's. In Jesus' words in the Gospel of Mark, "those who want to save their life will lose it, and those who lose their life for my sake, and for the sake of the gospel, will save it" (8:35).

Travel Log

Day 1:

Psalm 43 is a plea to God in the face of great difficulty. The psalmist seems to have been the subject of false accusations and public humiliation. It is the kind of prayer that Abraham and Sarah would have had the right to pray regarding their own state. Read the psalm aloud. As you read it, think of someone or some people who might be the victims of stigma or public humiliation. Note those people and/or groups of people in the space below and pray on their behalf.

Day 2:

Read and meditate upon Jesus' words in Mark 8:34-36. Write your thoughts or questions about these verses in the space below.

Day 3:

Make a list of things that are of great value to you. Then take a few minutes to pray. Start by closing your fists and naming some of the things on your list. Then slowly open your fists and read the list again. Keep your hands open and ask God to give you wisdom in ordering your life.

Day 4:

From the list you made yesterday, choose a few items and write about them in terms of your worship to God. How do they help or hinder your worship? How might you need to reconfigure your relationship to that item?

Day 5:

Describe a time when you felt like you were "standing in agonizing tension" between God and something important to you. What were you feeling? How did you respond?

Day 6:

Write a few words or draw a picture to describe a time when God created chaos or disorder in your life.

Day 7:

Where you do see yourself in this story? With whom or what do you identify? How does it challenge, convict, or comfort you? Journal your thoughts below.

From Death-Dealing To Life-Giving

Scripture for lesson: Exodus 20:2-17

In the Declaration of Independence, we find this familiar assertion: "We hold these truths to be self-evident, that all men are created equal, that they are endowed by their Creator with certain unalienable Rights, that among these are Life, Liberty and the pursuit of Happiness…. whenever any Form of Government becomes destructive of these ends, it is the Right of the People to alter or to abolish it." The birth of the United States of America was framed as a liberation from the oppressive regime of British tyranny and became the flagship for a new world, a "city on a hill" founded upon freedom and democracy.

In 1830, slightly more than 53 years after the signing of the Declaration of Independence, President Andrew Jackson signed the Indian Removal Act, which resulted in the relocation of approximately 50,000 Indians from the eastern United States. Eleven thousand Cherokees made a 6-9 month trek through the winter to their final location west of the Mississippi River. Approximately 4000 members of the Cherokee tribe died on what has become known as the "Trail of Tears."

Alexis de Tocqueville arrived in New York in 1831 as a representative from the French Ministry of Justice to observe and report on the American prison system. While he had a great love for Jefferson and a deep interest in this American democracy experiment, he observed that both the Native and African Americans "occupy an equally inferior position in the country they inhabit; both suffer from tyranny" (*Slouching Toward Tyranny: Mass Incarceration, Death Sentences and Racism*, by Joseph B. Ingle).

At the center of Israel's story is the theme of liberation and freedom from oppressive regimes of tyranny. Once people achieve freedom, the question then becomes what are they free to do? Who will they be? How will they live?

> Why might it be important to listen to the perspective of someone else about us and our community? What can we learn by including both our achievements and our failures as we tell our stories?

Prep for the Journey

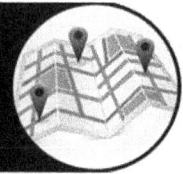

From what has God freed you? How did you react to your freedom?

In what ways has God provided for your most basic needs? How do you respond to God's provision?

The Book of Genesis ends with the Israelites living peacefully under the care of Joseph in Egypt, but with the turn of a page into the Book of Exodus, suddenly they are in peril, enslaved at the hands of an Egyptian king. Moses enters the story as God's chosen liberator for Israel, and he leads them out of the Egypt into the wilderness. The liberation celebration was short-lived and quickly turned into frustration with the Israelites declaring, "If only we had died by the hand of the LORD in the land of Egypt… for you have brought us into this wilderness to kill this whole assembly with hunger" (16:3). Freedom, it turns out, is not a walk in the park, but a painstaking trek through the desert.

God responded to the people's hunger by providing manna and quail (chapter 16), and their thirst by bringing water from a rock (chapter 17). In chapters 18 and 19 there was a move towards formalizing the nation's governance, and the people prepared for God's provision of the law. In Exodus 20:1-17, we find the Ten Commandments, which have such a central place in the life of the Israelites that the stone tablets on which they were carved resided in the Temple's holiest room, the Holy of Holies. The word *commandment* doesn't actually appear in the text; the directives are referred to as "the words" of God. A more accurate term is "the ten words" or "pronouncements." (Scholars also use the term *Decalogue*, which is the Greek for ten words.)

On the Road

On our journey through the pronouncements, we will visit its two distinct groups of verses. Our first stop will outline the Israelites' relationship to God; the second will deal with human relationships.

Read Exodus 20:2-7.

I am the LORD your God, who brought you out of the land of Egypt, out of the house of slavery; ³ you shall have no other gods before me.

⁴ You shall not make for yourself an idol, whether in the form of anything that is in heaven above, or that is on the earth beneath, or that is in the water under the earth. ⁵ You shall not bow down to them or worship them; for I the LORD your God am a jealous God, punishing children for the iniquity of parents, to the third and the fourth generation of those who reject me, ⁶ but showing steadfast love to the thousandth generation of those who love me and keep my commandments.

⁷ You shall not make wrongful use of the name of the LORD your God, for the LORD will not acquit anyone who misuses his name.

God doesn't do small talk. The voice of God means business. According to the Jewish Rabbinic tradition, the Israelites who were gathered at the foot of the mountain only heard verses 1 through 3. They were so terrified by the voice of God that they retreated from the mountain, leaving Moses as the mediator between them and God.

Verse 18 tells us that the people "were afraid and trembled and stood at a distance," fearing for their lives if God spoke to them. We don't know for sure how much or little the Israelites heard, but we can attempt to hear these words as if hearing them for the first time. If hearing the voice of the Divine wouldn't be terrifying enough, what that voice says would surely provoke a sense of reverence, awe, and perhaps, even holy terror. God insists upon being accepted, affirmed, and obeyed, and makes no apologies for being jealous. God had a passionate fidelity toward the Israelites, but would not tolerate unfaithfulness.

In the creation stories, God spoke the world into existence. On Mount Sinai, clouded by smoke and storm, God's voice was again central. The gods of other religions were made into visible objects that could be worshiped, such as statutes or structures, created by human hands and control. Many people profited from the making of these images.

These other gods could be seen, observed, and touched. The God of Israel, however, would not be domesticated by humans into an object. God will always remain a divine mystery beyond our full understanding and control.

Read Exodus 20:8-17.

Remember the sabbath day, and keep it holy. ⁹ Six days you shall labor and do all your work. ¹⁰ But the seventh day is a sabbath to the LORD your God; you shall not do any work—you, your son or your daughter, your male or female slave, your livestock, or the alien resident in your towns. ¹¹ For in six days the LORD made heaven and earth, the sea, and all that is in them, but rested the seventh day; therefore the LORD blessed the sabbath day and consecrated it.

¹² Honor your father and your mother, so that your days may be long in the land that the LORD your God is giving you.

¹³ You shall not murder.

¹⁴ You shall not commit adultery.

¹⁵ You shall not steal.

¹⁶ You shall not bear false witness against your neighbor.

¹⁷ You shall not covet your neighbor's house; you shall not covet your neighbor's wife, or male or female slave, or ox, or donkey, or anything that belongs to your neighbor.

How do you feel about hearing the voice of God? Why? How might you have reacted if you had been at the foot of the mountain?

How have you observed the name or idea of God being used for human gain or purpose? In what ways are we tempted to use God for our own gain or purpose? How do you respond to the idea of God as divine mystery beyond our control?

Revisit some of the ten pronouncements. How might they offer a new vision for the world than what the Israelites experienced in Egypt?

How do you observe the sabbath? How does ceasing from frantic productivity challenge you?

Would these six pronouncements alone be sufficient for a holy life? Why or why not? What would you add or remove? Which of these six are particularly challenging for our contemporary world?

The second group of verses begins with sabbath, which many of us think of as a day for worship. While certainly an appropriate response, worship is not the motivation for the practice of sabbath. Israel was to rest because God rested. God is not a workaholic. Ceasing from frantic productivity is at the heart of the divine, which challenges some of our own modern day idols and value commitments.

A brief glance through the Old Testament will tell you that Israel was going to have generational problems. They would forget and forsake their past, turning away from their religious tradition, practices, and worship. They would forget who they were, and how God had called them to be. They failed to remember that honoring one's father and mother is about respecting those who have gone before and led the way.

Verses 13 through 17 appear as cut and dry commands, but biblical scholar Lester Meyer points out that their simplicity raises endless questions. With regard to murder, for example: what about self-defense, abortion, war, or capital punishment? These ten are not intended to be an exhaustive list of Israel's Law. They are ten words or pronouncements that are less like a legal or religious checklist and more like a biblical vision for God's people. It is to that vision that we now turn.

Scenic Route

If you've ever responded to a parent by asking why, you've probably heard the words *because I told you so*. Maybe a parent has gotten you to do something by making you feel guilty, reminding you of things that he or she has done for you. There was undoubtedly an expectation that the Israelites would submit to the authority of God, and a sense of obligation for what God had done for them. However, we need to be careful not to miss something more central to the Israelite story and experience: liberation.

Read Exodus 20:2.

I am the LORD your God, who brought you out of the land of Egypt, out of the house of slavery.

The Israelites had been suffering in an Egyptian political regime that enslaved and oppressed them based upon their ethnicity. The pharaoh successfully created a division between Egyptian and Israelite, between "us" and "them," making one group believe that the other was dangerous. Seemingly, the only option was to crush "them" before they crush "us." Through fear and demonizing of the Israelites, the pharaoh created a political and social system that exploited a people group for his nation's gain. It was an economy of slavery in which the Israelites were a commodity to be used for the purpose of expanding and enlarging the Egyptian empire.

If the creation stories of Genesis paint the world as it ought to be, the slavery regime of Exodus provides the opposite. What God had given in abundance for all of creation became something to be exploited and extracted for the benefit of a few. This society was governed not by gratitude, but by greed and fear.

It is difficult to overstate the importance of Israel's experience of slavery because it was (and continues to be) so central to their faith story. They had known God as Creator, but now they have come to know God as Liberator. God brought them from death to life. Why then, almost as soon as they were freed, did the Israelites begin to wish they were still in Egypt? Maybe it was easier to accept the known realities of life in Egypt than to trust that the unknown would be better.

The Law, beginning with these ten pronouncements, was a vision of the way the world can and will be ordered under God. It is a new social reality, ordered around the God who liberates the powerless and gives hope to the hopeless. One biblical scholar describes the pronouncements as "a series of proclamations of how God should be practiced by liberated slaves." Another describes it as Israel's "freedom charter." Now that they have freedom from the death-dealing Egyptian slavery regime, the pronouncements and the law that will follow, free them to the life-giving order of God. The Law is not a burden under which to suffer, but a gift from which comes a life that gives joy and justice.

When have you found it more difficult to trust in future promises than accepting the reliability of the present? What happened? How did you feel about your decision?

What do we learn about God, ourselves, and the world from Israel's liberation? How is freedom understood by God and by Israel?

Workers Ahead

Moses led the people out of slavery in Egypt to ultimate freedom. We tend to forget that people are still enslaved, some even in our own country. Just recently I read about a woman who had been brought to this country to serve as a nanny for a wealthy family. She was beaten, kept as a prisoner, forced to beg and crawl in their home, and not given adequate food. Unfamiliar with this country and unable to speak English, this woman couldn't see a way out of her situation. She finally managed to get out of the house and wandered the streets until police found her. This all occurred in an upscale neighborhood in the United States.

We are appalled when we hear of animals being mistreated, as we should be, but sometimes it seems that we turn a blind eye to those things that enslave people. People are enslaved in many ways: Some

Of what types of enslavement are you aware? What are you willing to do to stop the enslavement of humans? How can you join with the efforts of others to work for freedom?

How has this lesson changed your view of God's Laws?

become trapped in the sex trade, while others are slaves in the cycle of poverty or to the drugs that have overtaken them. Migrant farm workers toil in the heat without water or rest breaks, and the list continues. Obviously, this list doesn't include the atrocities that happen in other countries where children are stolen, women raped and killed because they are thought to be dispensable, and Christians persecuted for expressing their faith.

Freedom is a gift that God intended for people. It's well past time the church took a stand and worked to free all of God's people.

In the Rear View

God freed the people of Israel from slavery in Egypt, but they were ill prepared to function as a nation. They had to learn that with freedom came responsibility to God and to others. God's gift of the Law was a way to help them identify these responsibilities and order their society.

It may be difficult for us to think in terms of laws as a gift from God, but without them the people would have been in chaos. Given the chaos of our world, it would seem helpful again to embrace God's gift. Only then can we truly be free.

Travel Log

Day 1:

Psalm 78 is a retelling of Israel's history. It begins by stating the importance of telling the story with the next generation, sharing both God's faithfulness and the people's unfaithfulness. Read the psalm aloud. As you read, imagine you are speaking to a crowd of people. Note words that stand out to you. Choose a couple of especially meaningful verses and write them in your own words in the space below.

Day 2:

Write about your own history and journey. What things do you remember and celebrate? What things do you regret and mourn? Why?

Day 3:

The Egyptian pharaoh successfully created division and fear by demonizing the Israelites. What divisions in our society are created by fear of others? How can you work to alleviate those fears? Make some notes below.

Day 4:

How will you observe the sabbath this week? Write down some ways that you can be intentional in taking the time for sabbath rest. If you are not currently observing sabbath time, you may need to start slowly and gradually increase your time.

Day 5:

   Whom do you know who is enslaved in some way? How can you reach out to that person in a way that offers a road to liberation?

Day 6:

   How do you view the laws of our country? In what ways are they a gift? a burden? Write your reflections below.

Day 7:
Write a prayer of gratitude for freedom and God's gift of the Law.

An Invitation to Be Set Apart

Scripture for Lesson:
1 Chronicles 29:1-9, 14-19

Monasticism was a religious movement that began in the fourth century shortly after Christianity became the official religion of the Roman Empire. The monastics, whom we know as monks, believed that Christianity was becoming corrupted by the world and joined communities of people who separated themselves from the world in order to be faithful to the gospel of Jesus. These communities were a way of life oriented around prayer, worship, work, and study.

In 1998, Shane Claiborne and five other Eastern University graduates founded The Simple Way community in Philadelphia, Pennsylvania. Like traditional monastics, this was a community ordered around prayer, worship, work, and study. However, rather than separating themselves from the world, they moved into a house in the poorest area of the city. Their goal was to set themselves apart for the work of God's kingdom in Philadelphia, first by living and sharing in community with one another, and then by engaging with the community around them.

These movements of Christianity are expressions of being set apart in the world to live a life ordered around the gospel of Jesus and in community with one another. They are perhaps the most socially extreme versions of what it means for Christians to live a life of "giving," and they will be helpful for us as we explore David's invitation to the Israelites.

How might your life and faith be impacted by living in this kind of community? How might this kind of separation be a help or a hindrance to living faithfully in an ever-changing society?

Prep for the Journey

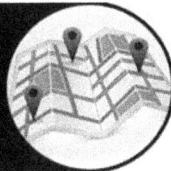

If you have managed to make your way through the historical books of Kings and Samuel, the first Book of Chronicles will feel like déjà vu. After nine chapters of detailed genealogies, you will again come across kings Saul, David, and Solomon, all of whose stories have been told previously. The Books of Chronicles, however, are an alternative telling of the information that precedes them—a different take on history.

Known only as "the chronicler," this mysterious writer's version of Israel's history places King David and the Jerusalem Temple on center stage. From the chronicler's perspective, David's vision and plan for the Temple was the crowning glory of Israel.

On the Road

David was the second king of Israel. Noticing that he had a fine home for himself but that God continued to "dwell" in a tent, David wanted to build a house for God. The actual construction of the Temple would be completed by his successor and son, Solomon, but David was the visionary, architect, and executive director. In this text he steps into the role of fund-raiser in what one scholar describes as "the mother of all capital fund campaigns." It was David's final task as king.

Read 1 Chronicles 29:1-5.

King David said to the whole assembly, "My son Solomon, whom alone God has chosen, is young and inexperienced, and the work is great; for the temple will not be for mortals but for the Lord God. ² So I have provided for the house of my God, so far as I was able, the gold for the things of gold, the silver for the things of silver, and the bronze for the things of bronze, the iron for the things of iron, and wood for the things of wood, besides great quantities of onyx and stones for setting, antimony, colored stones, all sorts of precious stones, and marble in abundance. ³ Moreover, in addition to all that I have provided for the holy house, I have a treasure of my own of gold and silver, and because of my devotion to the house of my God I give it to the house of my God: ⁴ three thousand talents of gold, of the gold of Ophir, and seven thousand talents of refined silver, for overlaying the walls of the house, ⁵ and for all the work to be done by artisans, gold for the things of gold and silver for the things of silver. Who then will offer willingly, consecrating themselves today to the Lord?"

So great a task was the building of the Temple that the nation's treasury could not meet the expense, nor could the king's personal wealth. This project would have bankrupted both David and Israel. This important task required the people's support if it was to be completed.

The king did not force the people to give, nor did he abuse his power and take from them. He did, however, ask more of them than simply their money or resources. The word *consecrate* means to set

When have you planned something only to have someone else implement it? How did you feel when that happened?

How do you feel about being asked to contribute support a major project? How does the way in which you are approached affect your response?

44

apart for a sacred purpose or holy service. The invitation from the king is to give one's whole self to the work and life of the Temple. The question is not "will you give your money, but will you give yourself?"

No doubt many congregations can identify with the daunting task of capital campaigns. Many of us have either despaired over the awkwardness of asking people to give, or fear being one who is asked to contribute. What we often miss in these discussions is a holistic vision and understanding of what it means to be engaged in the worshiping life of the church. In a fragmented culture, our worship life may easily become just one compartment of many. When that happens, we often become consumers of a religious product rather than people who are engaged in the life of a faith community. A consumer church asks its members to give money; a community of faith asks its members to give of themselves to one another, to worship, and to the mission of the church.

Read 1 Chronicles 29:6-9.

Then the leaders of ancestral houses made their freewill offerings, as did also the leaders of the tribes, the commanders of the thousands and of the hundreds, and the officers over the king's work. ⁷ They gave for the service of the house of God five thousand talents and ten thousand darics of gold, ten thousand talents of silver, eighteen thousand talents of bronze, and one hundred thousand talents of iron. ⁸ Whoever had precious stones gave them to the treasury of the house of the LORD, into the care of Jehiel the Gershonite. ⁹ Then the people rejoiced because these had given willingly, for with single mind they had offered freely to the LORD; King David also rejoiced greatly.

It was the kind of response about which churches and organizations dream. The people shared the vision and responded by giving generously. The giving involved all levels of the community from the king to the most humble family. It did not matter how much any single person gave, nor was it an occasion for celebrating one person over another. This effort united the people in a common cause. What mattered was that together they were able to accomplish their goal. The result was celebration for the whole community.

The quantities recorded are so extravagant that they are probably exaggerated amounts. The chronicler wanted to show just how important the Temple was to the life of Israel. It was more than the physical structure; it was the home of God and a symbol of Israel's worship, the heartbeat of their religious life. The Temple itself was not the object of their worship, but a symbol of their devotion to God. The building and the traditions that were enacted there were seen as acts of worship to God that demanded more than just half-hearted effort or commitment.

How can you be more than a consumer of a religious product? How difficult is it to give sacrificially of your money and time in a materialistic society?

How do you feel once a project is finished if you have been involved in its completion? if you did not participate? How important is the church to you? What does or does not make church worth your commitment?

How does your church invite its members to join in the work of the church?

How do you feel about those congregations whose buildings are elaborate and expensively decorated? Why?

Scenic Route

The celebration was followed by a time of thanksgiving, which David led. If any individual or even the community itself was tempted toward pride for its extravagant generosity, this prayer would have exposed those attitudes as illusions. David remembered that all life was a gift from God, the Creator. Rather than letting achievement sweep them up into a bloated ego, the tone of his prayer was one of confession, humbly recalling that people are tenants of a land that is not their own. They reap and sow, but it is the gift of God that gives life to the earth and sustenance to it all.

Read 1 Chronicles 29:14-17.

"But who am I, and what is my people, that we should be able to make this freewill offering? For all things come from you, and of your own have we given you. [15] For we are aliens and transients before you, as were all our ancestors; our days on the earth are like a shadow, and there is no hope. [16] O LORD our God, all this abundance that we have provided for building you a house for your holy name comes from your hand and is all your own. [17] I know, my God, that you search the heart, and take pleasure in uprightness; in the uprightness of my heart I have freely offered all these things, and now I have seen your people, who are present here, offering freely and joyously to you."

A life that is lived as a gift from God transforms giving from an act of human effort to an extension of God's grace. We are relinquishing what was never ours. This perspective is difficult to achieve in a world saturated with individualism that values people by what they earn and have. Giving our resources, especially our money, means to sacrifice some of that value, which can result in either reluctant giving or ulterior motives.

Intentions were clearly a matter of concern for David, but he was confident that all of the gifts would reflect willing and honest giving. There was no room for reluctance or greed in worship. This kind of confessional attitude brings the whole Temple project into perspective.

Workers Ahead

While the fundraising effort was the final act of David's reign, it was not the end of his concern. His reference to "the God of our fathers Abraham, Isaac, and Israel" recalls the faithfulness of God

How might thinking of your possessions as a gift from God change your attitude about giving?

Why does your community of faith exist? What does it do and why? What are its vision, hopes, dreams, and goals?

throughout history and anticipates its continuation into the future. In contrast, it would also have called to mind the unfaithfulness of the people and would have reminded them of the need for diligence in their commitment to God. David didn't just pray that Solomon would complete the construction of the Temple; he also asked that his son would remain devoted to the commands, statutes, and decrees.

Read 1 Chronicles 29:18-19.

"O LORD, the God of Abraham, Isaac, and Israel, our ancestors, keep forever such purposes and thoughts in the hearts of your people, and direct their hearts toward you. [19] Grant to my son Solomon that with single mind he may keep your commandments, your decrees, and your statutes, performing all of them, and that he may build the temple for which I have made provision."

A physical building does not constitute a faithful worshiping community; a people committed to way of life and worship is required. Being a faithful member of the religious community, as the chronicler saw it, meant to give oneself fully to its life and work. It requires the giving of resources, including finances, but also includes participation in worship, and the ordering of one's life around the ways of God.

When a person becomes a member of a congregation, he or she makes not only a profession of faith in Christ, but covenants to participate fully in the life of the faith community. The following are the questions that are generally asked of a person who desires to become a member of a Cumberland Presbyterian church:

Do you repent of your sin and believe Jesus Christ to be your Savior and the Lord of your life? Do you believe the scriptures of the Old and New Testaments to be the inspired word of God, the source of authority for faith and practice, and will you read and study them for guidance in living the Christian life? Do you promise to be a faithful member of this church by participating in worship, sharing in its ministry of witness and service, supporting the government of the Cumberland Presbyterian Church/Cumberland Presbyterian Church in America, and loving your brothers and sisters in Christ? Will you strive to overcome temptation and weakness, grow in knowledge and grace, and practice love in all relationships, being strengthened in your personal discipleship by your life in the community of faith? Do you promise to be a good steward of the life, talents, time, and money which God has entrusted to you, giving of these gifts to the church?

How are you reminded of your commitment to God?

What do these vows reveal about the church's expectations of its members? Which of these questions challenge you? Why?

In the Rear View

We began by examining a radical approach to Christianity wherein people set themselves apart from the world so that they could live in accordance with the gospel. We don't believe it is necessary to live physically apart from the world to serve God. However, David's vision for the people of Israel helps us understand that we set ourselves apart in the sense that we seek to follow God in every way, rather than living a life to which the world lures us. We must give our whole selves to a life oriented around the community of God. We covenant with God and our church to live a worshipful life in all parts of it, not just one compartment. Our lives are not our own, but a gift from God. We will only find the fullness of life when we are consecrated to the One who gave us life.

Travel Log

Day 1:

Imagine yourself approaching Jerusalem after the completion of the Temple. The city was set on a high hill, the Temple dominating the skyline. You would have been able to see the Temple long before arriving in the city, giving you plenty of time to reflect and prepare to worship.

Read Psalm 15. According to the psalmist, who can worship in the Temple? How do you feel about the psalmist's responses? What parts of the psalm resonate with you? Why? Journal your thoughts in the space below.

Day 2:

Not many people of faith choose to separate themselves from the rest of the world as do those who live in monastic communities, but faithful disciples structure their lives in ways through which they can draw closer to God. What habits or routines help you to stay rooted in God? What new habits or routines might you explore? Make note of these potential new practices. Review them in a few weeks to see your progress in implementing them.

Day 3:

Keeping in mind that *consecrate* means to be set apart for a sacred purpose, what changes do you need to make in your life so that you are truly consecrated to God? As you reflect on this question, journal your thoughts.

Day 4:

Make a list of the current needs of your faith community. How might the needs be met from within the current membership? What might God be calling you to contribute?

Day 5:

   Make a list of your gifts, abilities, and resources. With open hands, pray, listen, and discern the ways through which God wants to use your life in service to God's kingdom.

Day 6:

   Think of some people in your community of faith who seem to have set themselves apart, fully committed to God and the mission of the church. What about those individuals makes an impression, encourages, or convicts you? Write or draw your response.

Day 7:

Re-read the five promises from the Cumberland Presbyterian *Confession of Faith*. If you have made these promises, how faithful have you been in fulfilling them? Make some notes about ways in which you can improve or questions that have arisen.

Worrying the Kingdom Away

Scripture for Lesson:
Matthew 6:19-21, 25-34

A 2015 report from the American Psychological Association (APA) stated the following: "The United States is the world's richest country, with a gross domestic product nearly double that of the runner-up, yet our economic inequality is among the highest in the world. The Great Recession may have officially ended, but most American households face stagnant wages and increasing debt—many Americans are actually considered to be poorer than they were a decade ago."

Although the study found that stress levels in America overall were on a downward trend, money and finances were unsurprisingly among the top stressors. Nearly 72 percent of adults reported feeling stressed about money at least some of the time; 22 percent of those adults were experiencing extreme stress. Millennials and Gen Xers reported higher levels of financial stress, as did those households earning less than $50,000 per year.

As the already vast income equality gap in the United States continues to increase, the ideal of the American dream is fast becoming a myth for younger generations. New generations are having to ask what the pursuit of happiness looks like as they consider how to live their lives.

Prep for the Journey

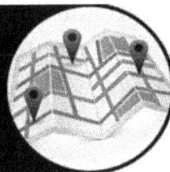

According to Matthew's Gospel, Jesus' public ministry began with a proclamation: "Repent, for the kingdom of heaven has come near" (4:17). The word *repent* means to turn around, to go in a new direction. Jesus declared that God had drawn close, that the gap between heaven and earth had narrowed and was being made known. The presence of God was being revealed in the man Jesus, beckoning people then and now to repent, to turn around and go in a new direction. The question is: In what direction are we to go?

> What causes you to be stressed? How do you deal with the stress?

> What does a life lived in the reality of God's kingdom look like?

How can you give hope to those who have none? What ministries of your faith community address this concern?

Where do you invest your time, energy, and resources? What parts of those investments do you need to re-evaluate?

The Sermon on the Mount is a lengthy episode of Jesus' teaching. Having only recently called his first disciples, Jesus began to teach what it meant to be participants in the kingdom of God. It soon became evident that Jesus' teachings were different from those of the religious leaders. Jesus was concerned with the needs of those who were "the least of these," to whom many of these statements were addressed. "Blessed are the poor in spirit… those who mourn… the hungry… the persecuted."

Jesus' teachings lifted up those who were thought to be unimportant. Heaven had drawn near, and the idea of what it meant to be blessed began to take on a whole different meaning. Jesus gave hope to those who had had none.

On the Road

The culture at the time, which was not unlike our own, valued physical possessions above other things. A person who had great wealth was treated with more respect and deference, and was generally thought of as being more important than those who had less. Sound familiar?

Read Matthew 6:19-21.

"Do not store up for yourselves treasures on earth, where moth and rust consume and where thieves break in and steal; 20 but store up for yourselves treasures in heaven, where neither moth nor rust consumes and where thieves do not break in and steal. 21 For where your treasure is, there your heart will be also.

Jesus knew that people invest their time, energy, and resources in the things they value most. He also knew that those things were only temporary and could be lost at a moment's notice. The challenge was in getting people to understand that they needed to focus on God rather than worry about their worldly needs, wants, and possessions.

Read Matthew 6:25-34.

"Therefore I tell you, do not worry about your life, what you will eat or what you will drink, or about your body, what you will wear. Is not life more than food, and the body more than clothing? 26 Look at the birds of the air; they neither sow nor reap nor gather into barns, and yet your heavenly Father feeds them. Are you not of more value than they? 27 And can any of you by worrying add a single hour to your span of life? 28 And why do you worry about clothing? Consider the lilies of the field, how they grow; they neither toil nor spin, 29 yet I tell you, even Solomon in all his glory was not clothed like one of these. 30 But if God so clothes

the grass of the field, which is alive today and tomorrow is thrown into the oven, will he not much more clothe you—you of little faith? [31] *Therefore do not worry, saying, 'What will we eat?' or 'What will we drink?' or 'What will we wear?'* [32] *For it is the Gentiles who strive for all these things; and indeed your heavenly Father knows that you need all these things.* [33] *But strive first for the kingdom of God and his righteousness, and all these things will be given to you as well.*

[34] *"So do not worry about tomorrow, for tomorrow will bring worries of its own. Today's trouble is enough for today.*

Being told "don't worry" is rarely, if ever, a helpful response. It neither deals with the problem nor suggests a solution. Jesus at least offered a reason why we should not worry, pointing to nature as evidence of God's care for the creation, arguing that if God cares for the birds of the air and the lilies of the field, would not God care even more for humans? The vivid imagery paints a beautiful picture of God's provision for creation, yet it also may feel idealistic and unrealistic. This is another tension of faith with which followers of Jesus often struggle.

Many Americans worry on a regular basis. Some of those worries are major concerns such as finding jobs, housing, cures for chronic and fatal diseases, etc. Other concerns may not seem as significant, but to some people they are just as important. Is this job the right one for me? Is my child developing appropriately? When am I going to find time to mow the lawn? Am I gaining weight? What will my parents/spouse/friends think?

Jesus didn't mean that those things about which we worry aren't important. In fact, Jesus said of food, water, and clothes that "your heavenly Father knows that you need all these things" (6:32). Nor is it that we shouldn't ask for God's provision, as Jesus taught us to pray for "our daily bread" (6:11). It's that in investing our energy and resources on these things, they become our "treasures on earth" and where our "heart will be also" (6:19, 21). We may worry so much because we have so many things about which we are concerned.

Participation in God's kingdom requires a reorientation of the heart and of our priorities. "You cannot serve two masters," Jesus said (6:24). We cannot invest our energies in serving God's kingdom when they are bound in anxiety and fear. We cannot be full participants in God's kingdom when we are preoccupied with worldly issues. Choosing God's kingdom over our own wants does not mean we ignore the things that concern us, but that we refuse to allow our worries to control us.

Take, for example, the stress of worrying about how to pay the bills, which is a legitimate concern. Worry in this sense acts as a helpful alarm, telling us that we need to take action, perhaps looking for a second or new job—or widening our search for any job—or reducing our spending. This concern may be so important that it causes sleepless nights, puts stress on relationships, and starts to preoccupy our thoughts, making it difficult to focus on anything else. When that happens, we begin to operate out of a place of fear, tension, and an inability to be present to people, the world around us, or God.

What causes you to feel anxious? If you had been in the crowd to which Jesus was preaching, what might your response have been to his statement about nor worrying?

If you had fewer things, would your worry be less? Why or why not? How does remembering God's promised provision of those things that are necessary for our survival lessen your worry?

Think of a time when you were particularly worried about something. How did the worry affect your thinking or behavior? What are some positive aspects about worrying? What are some characteristics of unhealthy worry? How might your thinking need to change in order to be attentive to God's kingdom rather than your own?

What is the world like when people view it as a place of scarcity? When have you experienced that attitude? How do you feel about sharing your resources? What are some obstacles to your giving?

How have you experienced the lightening of worry by giving to others?

When have you witnessed something akin to the making of stone soup? How might your giving contribute in a way similar to that of the villagers?

It would be harmful to say that someone shouldn't worry about financial stress, but it is impossible to be open to the grace, presence, and call of God when we become so invested and lost in worry. Instead of living from a place of fear, disciples are to live out of a radical commitment to the call of God, trusting that God will provide for them. This section of the sermon is summed up in the final verses when Jesus said, "strive first for the kingdom of God and his righteousness, and all these things will be given to you as well" (verse 33).

Scenic Route

Worry is essentially a fear of losing something—financial security, a job, a relationship, or even life. Worry generally manifests itself when something of value to us is threatened. We often respond to the threat by trying to protect what we consider to be valuable. We put our energies into protecting it and build defenses against the threat—real or perceived. To worry is to fear that the world is not a hospitable place, but a hostile place of scarcity in which we need to take what we can and defend it against others.

When we spend time worrying, we have lost that time and caused ourselves to suffer. Giving to others when we are wrapped up in our own concerns is almost impossible. We have to learn to let go of our own worries and needs so that we can reach outside of ourselves. When we do, we are likely to discover that others will share our burdens as we share theirs. Looking for ways to give to others diminishes our own worries and helps us to focus on God's kingdom.

Consider the story of stone soup as you contemplate the idea of scarcity in your life: Some travelers came to a village, carrying only an empty cooking pot. Upon their arrival, the villagers were unwilling to share any of their food stores with the hungry travelers. Then the travelers went to a stream and filled the pot with water, dropped a large stone in the pot, and placed it over a cooking fire. One of the villagers became curious and asked what they were doing. The travelers answered that they were making a wonderful dish called "stone soup," but that they still needed a few ingredients to improve the flavor. The villager did not mind parting with a few carrots to help them out. When another villager inquired about the pot, the travelers again mentioned their stone soup, which had not reached its full potential. The villager handed them a little bit of seasoning. More and more villagers walked by, each adding another ingredient. Finally, the stone (being inedible) was removed from the pot, and a delicious and nourishing pot of soup was enjoyed by all. By sharing the limited amounts of food that each person had, the villagers were able to make a nourishing meal for everyone.

Workers Ahead

Life in God's kingdom is characterized by a radical trust that God has and will continue to provide for the creation. It is to believe in abundance rather than scarcity, in sharing rather than hoarding, in giving rather than taking. Instead of building storehouses and fences to protect ourselves and those things we value, it is a life with doors open to neighbors and strangers.

Choosing to believe and live in God's abundance frees us from destructive patterns of living and opens us up to the presence and call of God. It also allows us to enter a life of giving. Like most of Jesus' teachings, it is not a simple path, does not always make sense in our world, and will only be achieved with great faith and struggle.

In the Rear View

In light of the APA report referenced at the beginning of this lesson, Jesus' teachings are not easy for us to hear. It may feel like a world of abundance for a few and of scarcity for the many.

Millard Fuller, founder of Habitat for Humanity International, believed that we were called to create a greater balance between those who had an abundance of resources and those who were lacking. He argued that the resources exist throughout the world to eliminate substandard housing globally. The question, he said, is whether or not people have the will to change. The same argument could be made for food and clothing. One way in which God provides for those in need is by working through the hearts of those who have enough.

Jesus' teachings open for us a new way to see and live in the world. Jesus helped people then (and now) to believe that a new reality was possible, one in which life was abundant because of dependence on God rather than on our material, economic, or social successes. Have you ever witnessed the overwhelming joy and generosity extended by some people who seem to have so few possessions—especially compared to many Americans? Jesus invites us to be very present in each moment rather than spending our lives looking to tomorrow. Jesus reminds us to be present before God and in relationship to those around us, rather than wrapped up in ourselves. Finally, Jesus invites us to live as people who give, share, and serve—as people whose priority is God's kingdom.

How willing are you to believe Jesus' claim that God can and will provide for your needs abundantly? What would allow you to give of yourself and your resources more freely?

Travel Log

Day 1:

Psalm 46 is a bold declaration of trust in God. Even when the foundations of the earth were shaken, the psalmist said the people would not be afraid because God was their refuge. Think about times when you have sought refuge in God. How did God give you the assurances that you needed? Write a few words or sentences of reflection.

Day 2:

In the space below, list those things about which you are anxious. Beside each one note the reason for your anxiety. Then write or say a simple prayer in response to each one.

Day 3:

Describe a time when you were especially worried about something. About what were you worried? How did you feel? How did you respond? How did your behavior change as a result of the anxiety?

Day 4:

In what ways do you see the world as a place of scarcity? of abundance? Reflect as to how your views influence your choices and the ways you live.

Day 5:

We build fences around those people and things that we are worried we might lose. In doing so, we keep others out, closing both ourselves and our resources off to the world. What resources do you fear losing? How does your fear impact the way in which you respond to others?

Day 6:

Who in your life seems overburdened by fears and anxieties? How can you share his or her burdens? How is sharing someone's burdens a way of sharing abundance?

Day 7:

What do Jesus' teachings about worry and providing mean for your life? Make some notes or draw as you reflect about those teachings.

Source

"Stress in America: Paying with our Health." American Psychology Association, February 4, 2015. Web. https://www.apa.org/news/press/releases/stress/2014/stress-report.pdf

Giving God an Ear

Scripture for lesson: Mark 4:21-25

What do you think the Zen master meant? What "cup" do you need to empty?

Theologian Henri Nouwen tells a story about a university professor who came to a Zen master to ask him about Zen. When Nan-in, the Zen master, served some tea, he poured until the professor's cup was full, and then continued to pour.

The professor watched the overflow until he could no longer restrain himself. "It is over-full. No more will go in!"

"Like this cup," Nan-in said, "you are full of your own opinions and speculations. How can I show you Zen unless you first empty your cup?"

(Excerpt taken from Henri Nouwen's *Spiritual Formation: Following the Movements of the Spirit.*)

Prep for the Journey

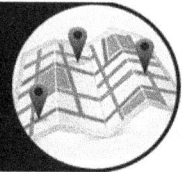

The Gospel According to Mark is the gospel in a hurry. At only 16 chapters, it's shorter than the other three Gospels. Mark's account may be appealing to readers because of its conciseness, which cuts to the chase and highlights the action. One could easily make the mistake of assuming the brevity of Mark reflects its simplicity. In reality, the truth may be exactly the opposite.

The Gospels of Matthew and Luke contain lengthy, though differing, narratives about Jesus' birth. They both start with an angelic announcement to people who couldn't possibly be parents because they had not yet had sex. Immediately we see that the arrival of Jesus was extraordinary, an act of God. These Gospel writers went out of their way to tell the reader who Jesus is. Matthew says that Jesus is "God with us" (1:23), a king who is a threat to existing rulers such as Herod (2:3), and revered by foreign astronomers (2:10). According to Luke, Jesus is "Son of God" (1:35), the "Lord's Messiah" (2:26), and "a light for revelation to the Gentiles and for glory to [God's] people Israel" (2:32).

John's Gospel does not include a birth narrative, but begins with a poem in which he states that Jesus was not only sent from God, but was one with God.

In Mark, Jesus more or less just showed up while John was preaching and baptizing at the Jordan River. We still have a voice from heaven saying, "You are my son, the Beloved" (1:11), but we don't have nearly the same emphasis on who Jesus is or from where he came. In the stories Mark related, Jesus doesn't seem to have wanted people to know his identity. Jesus rebuked an unclean spirit who identified him (1:25), cautioned those who had been healed not to tell anyone (1:44), and sternly ordered others "not to make him known" (3:12).

On the Road

Why might Jesus have not wanted people to know his identity? How could that lack of knowledge have been to his benefit? When have you preferred to remain out of the spotlight? Why?

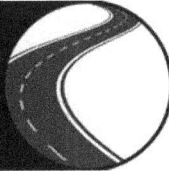

In contrast to the other three Gospels, this one seems to present Jesus as more of a mystery. It is this idea of the mystery of Jesus and of God's kingdom that will be the key to unlocking our text.

Read Mark 4:21-25.

He said to them, "Is a lamp brought in to be put under the bushel basket, or under the bed, and not on the lampstand? 22 For there is nothing hidden, except to be disclosed; nor is anything secret, except to come to light. 23 Let anyone with ears to hear listen!" 24 And he said to them, "Pay attention to what you hear; the measure you give will be the measure you get, and still more will be given you. 25 For to those who have, more will be given; and from those who have nothing, even what they have will be taken away."

When we come across what seem to be Jesus' more cryptic teachings, we tend to gravitate toward what makes sense. In this case, we are likely to focus on verse 24, which we can more easily understand.

Jesus seems to have been talking about generosity. Rather than focusing on gathering up treasure for ourselves, we are urged to be people who give because God rewards generosity. But if this is the case, what do we do with verse 25?

Chapter 4 begins with the parable of the sower. When Jesus was finished teaching, the disciples asked him about the parable. Apparently we are not the only ones who often have difficulty understanding what Jesus meant. Jesus, however, seemed quite satisfied that the meaning of the parables wasn't clear. He explained, "Everything comes in parables in order that they may look but not perceive, listen

How have you understood this teaching of Jesus? What, if anything, bothers you about it?

How do you seek understanding when something is not clear? When have others sought clarification about something you said or did? How did you feel about their need for clarification?

When and how has the teaching of Jesus and the kingdom of God challenged the way you see the world? When have you heard the teaching of Jesus in a way that led to real transformation in your thinking and behavior?

How do you feel about this interpretation of the parable? How can you give generously of your ear and mind? To whom will you give those gifts?

but not understand" (4:11-12). The kingdom of God, according to Mark's reporting of the life and teachings of Jesus, is a "secret" that has been revealed to the disciples (4:11), but the rest of the people are left to unlock the mystery.

It's not that Jesus didn't want people to know. After all, who brings a lamp out and puts it under something? (4:21). If the knowledge of God's kingdom is meant to be disclosed and made known (4:22), why does it seem as if Jesus was covering the lamp?

Remember that Jesus had just finished telling a parable about seeds. The "good seed" represents those who "hear the word and accept it and bear fruit" (4:20). The other seeds heard the word, but they did not receive it. So when Jesus beckoned, "Let anyone with ears to hear listen" (4:23), he was really wanting people to pay attention. Most of us are fortunate enough to have the physical ability to hear. In one sense, this command calls all people to listen, but Jesus was also pointing toward something else.

For those listening to Jesus who had the ability to hear, their eardrums were sending signals to their brains, which interpreted them. But receiving Jesus' teaching requires more than audio signals. It requires an openness to God, to a new way of seeing the world and new ways of being in it. It requires a rewiring of the imagination to be shaped around the values of God's kingdom rather than those of the world. It requires reorienting our hearts to desire the things that are at the heart of God.

Scenic Route

Re-read Mark 4:24-25.

And he said to them, "Pay attention to what you hear; the measure you give will be the measure you get, and still more will be given you. 25 For to those who have, more will be given; and from those who have nothing, even what they have will be taken away."

Now that we've been attentive to the context of the verses and we understand the importance of hearing in chapter 4, we can approach verses 24 and 25 with a new perspective. Jesus was not talking about generosity in terms of possessions, but a generosity of the ear and of the mind. To those who create space in their thinking and understanding, more insight will come, but to those who have no openness to God, the little understanding they do have will be taken from them.

Perhaps the reason for the mysterious, cryptic nature of Jesus in Mark's Gospel, is that God's kingdom is not merely a matter of doing what Jesus says. If it were, surely Jesus would have just plainly taught what was expected of his followers. But Jesus taught in parables that were (and are) often difficult to understand, particularly when it comes to teaching about God's kingdom. Time and time again Jesus said, "The kingdom is like…," telling parable after parable as if trying to give people a variety of examples, hoping that they would find at least one to which they could relate. We get the feeling that the kingdom of God simply cannot be explained in words, but only through similes, metaphors, parables, and actions.

If Jesus were teaching and living on earth now, our religious leaders might respond in ways very similar to the religious leaders of his day. Jesus' failure to give theologically clear and concise answers frustrated and angered the religious leaders. They saw things in very black and white terms: If it didn't fit within their interpretation of the Law and the prophets, it was wrong. Jesus' teachings challenged their view and made them uncomfortable.

We are drawn to those things that offer certainty—things that make sense in our minds and that we can express with our mouths. Jesus does not offer easy answers or simple steps, but invites us to have a radical openness to God's voice and kingdom, drawing us into a mystery that we can never pin down.

Workers Ahead

Have you ever been talking with someone, only to realize he or she wasn't hearing you? Maybe the person was distracted by something or someone else. Or perhaps the person was listening, but somehow completely missed your point. Worse, maybe the person interrupted you, assuming knowledge of what you were going to say.

Listening is a skill at which not all of us are good because it requires active engagement. Some people are better able to focus on another person and ask questions to engage him or her, but it takes effort and a desire to communicate. We must pay attention to the words that someone is saying to understand exactly what is being said and why the words are being uttered. It means giving the other person our full attention because the words are their words, not ours. The speaker is expressing his or her thoughts, feelings, and ideas—not ours.

One of the greatest barriers to effective communication is an inability to see, think, or talk about the world in a way other than our own. We presume that everyone should operate within our parameters. This psychological understanding wasn't around in Jesus' day, but it sure seems that Jesus had a firm grasp on most humans' inability to listen.

What is your comfort level with the idea of mystery? What keeps you from having an openness to God's voice and kingdom?

When are you guilty of hearing but not listening? How do you feel when you sense that someone is not truly listening to you?

What interferes with your being a good listener? What practices help you to pay attention to God's voice and kingdom? What other practices might also be helpful?

Just as listening to other people effectively takes work, commitment, and love, so does listening to God. We must not assume that we already know what God thinks, wills, or wants. God doesn't necessarily value the same things that we do. We cannot finish God's sentences, assuming that we know how God will respond.

If we are to "give ear to God," we must train ourselves to pay attention, listen, and create a space in which we can open ourselves up to the new possibilities of God's voice and kingdom.

In the Rear View

Many of us—like the religious leaders in Jesus' day—come to religion with a cup full of ideas, images, beliefs, and assumptions. The contemporaries of Jesus took great pride in knowing the scriptures and the Law, which did not leave room for Jesus or his teachings. When our cup is full, we feel no need for more, no need to listen.

But Jesus says, pay attention! For those who open their ears, minds, and hearts to the mystery of God and God's kingdom, the secrets will continue to unfold.

Travel Log

Day 1:

Make a list of the ways you can recall Jesus describing the kingdom of God/heaven. Do an Internet search if you need help. Which example resonates the most with you? Why?

Day 2:

In the blank space below, draw a cup. Inside the cup write a prayer of confession, naming the things that interfere with your listening attentively to God.

Day 3:

The people to whom Jesus spoke had a choice as to whether or not to believe his teachings. If they did believe, they had to make some major adjustments.

How has coming to know Christ caused you to think, believe, or act differently? Make a list of things that you used to think, believe, or do and write beside it how your attitudes, beliefs, and actions have changed.

Day 4:

Reflect about your faith journey. Recall a time when following Jesus caused you to make a radical change. Write about this time.

Day 5:

One of the most important gifts we can give to others is listening. Think of someone who might need a listening ear. How can you reach out to that person? Write down a few questions that could help you start the conversation. Then call the person.

Day 6:

Instead of talking to God in prayer, try spending a few minutes listening to God in prayer. You may find it helpful to repeat silently a word or phrase in rhythm with your breathing to keep you from being distracted by other thoughts. (For example, when breathing in, repeat, "Let your kingdom come." As you breathe out, repeat, "Let your will be done.")

Day 7:

Reflect on your day. Remember the people you met, the work you did, the food you ate, the sites you visited, and the profiles you browsed. What might God have been saying to you throughout the day? What did you notice about how God might have been at work? At what points may you have been joining with God's efforts? Ask God to guide your thinking and reflecting.

The Widow's Plight: Giving Attention to The Poor

Scripture for Lesson: Mark 12:38-44

The Rev. Lisa Cook was ordained by the Cumberland Presbyterian Church in January 2014, for ministry as a chaplain to the homeless community in Nashville, Tennessee. A few months earlier, she had become the founder of Sacred Sparks Ministry. During the winter months when the temperatures are dangerously low, Sacred Sparks works with a local Cumberland Presbyterian church to provide an emergency shelter where up to 30 adults (plus pets) can go to get out of the cold, have a place to rest, and a hot meal. Through the donations of the building, cots, clothes, and food, this ministry has offered protection to some of Nashville's most vulnerable residents.

Glance through Lisa's social media and you'll see that the work extends beyond the winter months. Every Wednesday there's the group trip to the laundromat, complete with transportation and quarters for the washers and dryers provided by Sacred Sparks volunteers and supporters. Sacred Sparks also provides transportation for trips to visit family members, help in acquiring identification cards, and Bible studies in the park.

Providing for the physical and material needs of people who are homeless is important, but it is the last of the three Sacred Sparks goals: being present and building relationships with our friends in the homeless community; providing real opportunities for spiritual growth through worship, study, and pastoral care; providing outreach and basic necessities for survival, shelter, and well-being.

Though her ministry is based in the tented communities throughout the city rather than a church, homeless people are Rev. Cook's congregation. Like all congregations, they need the love and support of a community, but they are also invited to become disciples and serve in the body of Christ.

For more information about Sacred Sparks, go to https://sacredsparksministry.wordpress.com/.

How does your faith community respond to people who are homeless? What can people who are homeless give to the kingdom of God?

Prep for the Journey

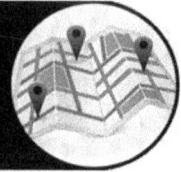

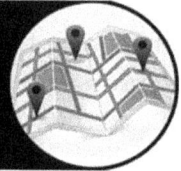

Scholars have determined that Mark's Gospel was the first one to have been written. It is also the shortest of the Gospel accounts. With no birth narrative, Jesus burst onto the scene after a brief introduction by his cousin John. The remainder of the story of Jesus' life is narrated in brief, concise terms. The key theme of this Gospel is Jesus' proclamation that "the kingdom of God is at hand." Mark is much less concerned with Jesus the person than with how his actions revealed God's kingdom entering the world.

The story of the widow's offering at the Temple is found in both Mark and Luke. In Mark's Gospel, this visit to the Temple was Jesus' last public appearance before Judas betrayed him to the authorities. While at the Temple, the religious leaders challenged Jesus' authority, theology, and controversial teachings.

> **When has someone challenged your authority, theology, or teachings? How did you react?**

Prep for the Journey

In the very place where the priests, scribes, and elders most often exercised their power and authority, Jesus told a parable, which they realized was directed at them. Though they wanted to arrest Jesus, he had attracted such a crowd of people that arresting him would have just caused more problems. Unintimidated, Jesus continued to engage various groups of people, all the while drawing the interest and delight of a large crowd.

Read Mark 12:38-40.

As he taught, he said, "Beware of the scribes, who like to walk around in long robes, and to be greeted with respect in the marketplaces, ³⁹ and to have the best seats in the synagogues and places of honor at banquets! ⁴⁰ They devour widows' houses and for the sake of appearance say long prayers. They will receive the greater condemnation."

Still standing in the Temple, Jesus continued to speak out against many of its religious leaders, this time specifically the scribes, many of whom were also Pharisees. Scribes were responsible for the preservation, study, and interpretation of the Law of Moses. They also taught the Law to groups of students or disciples.

Jesus wasn't condemning the Jewish religion; he was, after all, a faithful Jew. What Jesus condemned was the misuse of religious authority for the purpose of power and status. The scribes were

> **What groups of people might Jesus be describing in today's world? How does the church continue to speak out against these types of injustices?**

supposed to be serving God and God's people, but instead they used their position of power and authority to serve themselves.

We know all too well in our contemporary world that ministers are not immune to the lure of their egos. Television shows that feature celebrity pastors reveal this lack of immunity at its most obvious, but special treatment of the clergy is not limited to celebrities. Given how much time clergy people spend as the center of attention and that they are often viewed as authority figures and given special honor, it is inevitable that most clergy people have to work at keeping their egos in check.

Avoiding religious arrogance may be particularly pertinent to clergy, but it is an issue that is by no means limited to them. They are certainly not the only people who are tempted to use religion for the sake of appearance, status, or gain. We are to beware of those people because their "religion" is rooted in something other than God. It may be in the guise of God, and may even be something good like prayer or giving, but its intention is self-serving. When a religious expression is something other than a sincere and faithful response to God, it has the potential to be destructive.

Read Mark 12:41-44.

He sat down opposite the treasury, and watched the crowd putting money into the treasury. Many rich people put in large sums. ⁴² A poor widow came and put in two small copper coins, which are worth a penny. ⁴³ Then he called his disciples and said to them, "Truly I tell you, this poor widow has put in more than all those who are contributing to the treasury. ⁴⁴ For all of them have contributed out of their abundance; but she out of her poverty has put in everything she had, all she had to live on."

The Temple had 13 treasury boxes that were located in one of the outer courts, which made them accessible to all those who visited the Temple. Some artists depict these receptacles as having a trumpet-shaped tube that emptied into a wooden box or chest. These boxes were for the purpose of collecting funds that supported the Temple.

With no online giving, checks, or paper money, the size of the contribution would have been easy for even a casual observer to determine. Imagine spotting a wealthy donor approach the treasury with a bag of coins in hand. As he places the coins in the metal tube, they make a noticeable sound. Like the coin hitting the bottom of a charity collector's bucket, the sound confirms to both the giver and to those around that the donation has been made, and gives us a clue to the amount of the donation.

Holding only two small coins, the widow's contribution would have taken only a moment and would have barely made a sound when it was dropped into the box. Perhaps she was scorned, pitied, or just ignored by those around the treasury. It may be that she approached while no one else was around so as to go unnoticed. What we do know is that amidst many large contributions, Jesus made note of her seemingly insignificant one.

How do the comments about clergy people change your view of those who serve in this way? How might it change your interactions and relationships with members of the clergy?

In what ways might you be religiously arrogant? How have you experienced religion being misused for personal gain?

When have you noticed the amount of someone's gift? What drew your attention to it? How did you react to the person's gift?

What is your response to Jesus' preference for the widow's offering? How does this example challenge or encourage your attitude about giving?

How do you imagine people would have treated the scribes, the wealthy, and the poor widow? How are similar groups of people treated today?

In one congregation, a family who made large donations was automatically always represented on the session. How is the power in your faith community distributed?

In the first-century world, a male head of household was imperative for the honor and provision of a family. A widow was not just someone who had lost a spouse; she had also lost a protector and provider. Any widow was vulnerable, but a poor widow faced a nearly hopeless task of survival. The actual amount of the offering made by the widow in this story was much less than that of the wealthy donors, but the cost she paid dwarfed theirs. Her donation was not just equal with that of the wealthy donors, but it was of greater value because she gave all she had and they gave from their abundance.

Scenic Route

In many Bibles, readers will find a heading such as "Jesus Denounces the Scribes" above verse 38, followed two verses later by "The Widow's Offering." Because of this division, we tend to view the stories separately; however, they were intended to be read together. By considering the stories together, we see that Jesus linked together the scribes, wealthy people, and the poor widow. We are meant to read the widow's story in light of Jesus' warning about following the scribes. Jesus portrayed the widow as being faithful and having no power to wield, no reputation for prominence, and virtually nothing to give.

In many churches, making a large donation results in significant power and influence in the operation of the congregation. It can include acknowledgments such as the naming of buildings, the dedication of windows, or even public announcements. While it may be appropriate to acknowledge significant gifts, surely what Jesus revealed is that those who give the most are not necessarily more authentic or significant than someone who gives far less. It would certainly be unfair to say that the gifts of wealthy people are of less value, but Jesus' observations should be cause to think critically about our attitudes toward giving.

There is one other crucial connection we miss when we read these two stories separately. In verse 40 Jesus accused the scribes of devouring widow's houses. Just a couple of verses later, a widow gave all she had. She did not know how she would provide for her own basic needs. The monetary needs of the Temple were supposed to have included care for those who were widowed, orphaned, or strangers.

The scribes were among the recipients of the Temple treasury. Their livelihood came from what people gave to the treasury, which in this case was from the emptying of a widow's pockets. Jesus implied that the scribes were so busy parading around at public functions that they were completely oblivious, or even intentionally ignorant, of the suffering of the vulnerable. In contrast, Jesus paid attention to the woman who had been ignored and her offering that would be overlooked. In doing so, he highlighted a corrupt system that abused those who were poor and vulnerable.

Workers Ahead

One of the primary duties of the Temple and of the Church is to care for those who are poor, widowed, orphaned, and sick. When a church's giving becomes disconnected from its mission, including a commitment to care for the vulnerable both inside and outside of the church, we stray from our calling as God's people.

When any organization strays from its mission, people become confused, disillusioned, and cease to support the work that was started. It is important to keep the mission in front of the people so that everyone is working together for the same purpose. Otherwise, groups and individuals will be setting their own priorities, which may not agree with those the organization established.

Every gift is important as evidenced in the following account:

Martha Chambers, a Cumberland Presbyterian who lives in Camden, Arkansas, has a gift for baking bread. When the Stott-Wallace Missionary Offering Fund was announced, Martha took to heart this challenge: "If 500 people or groups raised just $2,000 a year, the Cumberland Presbyterian Church would have one million dollars to support missionary work around the world." Using her gift, Martha started baking bread.

In a year's time, Martha had raised $2,000! She could have patted herself on the back for a job well done, but she got busy baking more bread and has now raised another $2,000 for the Stott-Wallace Missionary Offering Fund.

While our churches need funds to continue their ministry, some people, like the widow, are not able to support the church financially. However, they can make a contribution by volunteering their gifts and abilities. For instance, landscaping/mowing, doing maintenance work, volunteering in the office, serving as custodian, and so forth are all ways of contributing to the church's budget.

What situations in our world does this example parallel? How can you be more intentional in recognizing and assisting those who are poor and vulnerable?

How does your church use the funds that are entrusted to it? What percentage of the budget is dedicated to helping those who are vulnerable? How does or might your congregation or community engage in caring for those who are vulnerable?

What is the mission of your church? How are people made aware of the mission? How do the ministries and programs of your church reflect that mission?

What gift do you have that can be used to further God's work?

How can people contribute to your faith community's budget in non-monetary ways? How is appreciation for those contributions shown?

We can give thanks for the many nonprofit organizations that provide for the material needs of those who are poor and vulnerable. We should celebrate when our churches engage in acts of mercy and charity towards those who are in need. But Jesus revealed something that may be surprising and difficult to us. The poor are equally, if not more, capable of living faithfully than are those with wealth. They have gifts and resources to offer our communities. As the ministry of Sacred Sparks demonstrates, the Church has the potential to engage the poor as Jesus did, by giving them our attention and honoring their humanity.

Travel Log

Day 1:

What organizations in your community serve those who are homeless or vulnerable in other ways? How can you be supportive of their ministries? In what ways can you get involved? If no such organizations exist, consider how you and your church should respond to the needs in your community.

Make notes in the space below. Refer to them as you investigate the available resources.

Day 2:

Jesus took the time to sit and watch the people in his community, to pay attention, and to notice them. Take a walk or drive around your community, paying attention to the people. What groups of people are overlooked? What is the general attitude toward them? How might Jesus see them? Journal your thoughts as you reflect on the questions.

Day 3:

Everyone needs to feel valued. One way we can value another person is by taking the time to listen to his or her life story. Thinking of the people about whom you wrote yesterday, make a list of questions you could ask that would help you get to know them.

Day 4:

Write or draw about a time when you felt ignored, unheard, or unappreciated. What did it feel like?

Day 5:

Many people are uncomfortable talking about financial needs/responsibilities in conjunction with the church. How do you respond when an organization approaches you about making a contribution? How do you respond when you hear a sermon about tithing? Consider your responses and jot some notes as to why you feel this way.

Day 6:

The lesson asked participants what gifts they have that can be used for God's work. What gifts did you identify? List them here. Beside each gift, write one or more ways in which you use that gift to serve God.

Day 7:

Reflect about Jesus' teachings regarding giving. How do they challenge your attitude about money, those who are wealthy, and those who are poor? Journal your thoughts below.

Outrageous Generosity

Scripture for lesson: Luke 6:27-38

Pastor and author Brian McLaren tells the story of a white South African man's encounter with the influential black Anglican bishop Desmond Tutu during the apartheid regime. Bishop Tutu was an advocate and activist for the end of apartheid, and, in the eyes of this white man, was a heretic and a troublemaker. They were in an airport when the white man saw the bishop coming toward him. Filled with resentment, he deliberately stepped into Tutu's path, aggressively knocking the bishop to the floor.

Looking up at the man from the ground, Tutu could see the obvious intent and evil in the man's eyes. The bishop simply smiled at him and said, "God bless you, my child."

Surprised and angry, the man trudged away, leaving Tutu on the ground. He could not, however, shake the bishop's gracious and non-violent response to his aggression. His encounter with grace and love in spite of his hate became the catalyst for gradual repentance and his eventual conversion.

Prep for the Journey

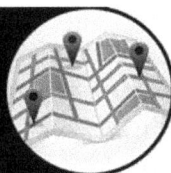

In Jesus' day, it was common for a teacher to have disciples or followers—those who embraced his teachings and thoughts. Luke tells us that after spending the night in prayer on a mountainside, Jesus chose 12 men from those who were already his followers. These 12 became his innermost circle, those to whom he eventually entrusted the furtherance of God's kingdom.

A crowd had gathered on a level area near the mountain, with some people waiting to hear Jesus teach and others hoping to be healed of diseases and unclean spirits. As he began to teach them, he announced four unusual blessings: Blessed are those who are poor, those who are hungry, those who weep, and those who are hated. He

> What is your usual response when someone intentionally causes your harm? What do you think of Bishop Tutu's response? How might it have served as a catalyst for the man's repentance?

followed the statement of blessings with four opposite statements, equally surprising: Woe to those who are rich, those who are full, those who laugh, and those of whom people speak well.

It's hard to imagine too many times or cultures in which these words would not be entirely and radically contrary to the norm. We often think and speak of blessings in terms of a life that is materially, socially, emotionally, and spiritually comfortable or stable. In the teaching of Jesus, these things do not equal blessings. In fact, Jesus declared them to be a curse. The blessed are those who are deprived of such things.

Having challenged our vision of what a blessed life looks like, Jesus turned his attention to how a blessed life should be lived, which was no less shocking.

On the Road

Jesus obviously meant for this teaching to be very personal as he used the words *you* or *your* 32 times in the 12 verses being considered in this lesson. (Ten of the verses are printed in this section. You will find the last two near the end of the lesson.) As was discussed in the previous lesson, not everyone who hears actually listens. The first *you* was an invitation to the listener, and is to us the reader, to pay close attention to Jesus' words.

Read Luke 6:27-31.
"But I say to you that listen, Love your enemies, do good to those who hate you, 28 bless those who curse you, pray for those who abuse you. 29 If anyone strikes you on the cheek, offer the other also; and from anyone who takes away your coat do not withhold even your shirt. 30 Give to everyone who begs from you; and if anyone takes away your goods, do not ask for them again. 31 Do to others as you would have them do to you.

Jesus began by asking his listeners to place themselves in a number of scenarios, each of which made them victims of others' abusive actions. These teachings are contrary to human nature. When someone takes or demands from us those things for which we have worked and paid, we expect something in return. When someone assaults us, physically or verbally, we want to strike back, but Jesus said to do just the opposite. We have heard these teachings, especially what has come to be known as "the golden rule," most of our lives. For those who were listening to Jesus that day, his teaching turned their world upside down.

How would you define "a blessed life"? Whom would you consider "not blessed"? Why?

What victims of injustice could be harmed if this text was wrongly used?

Read Luke 6:32-36.

"If you love those who love you, what credit is that to you? For even sinners love those who love them. ³³ If you do good to those who do good to you, what credit is that to you? For even sinners do the same. ³⁴ If you lend to those from whom you hope to receive, what credit is that to you? Even sinners lend to sinners, to receive as much again. ³⁵ But love your enemies, do good, and lend, expecting nothing in return. Your reward will be great, and you will be children of the Most High; for he is kind to the ungrateful and the wicked. 36 Be merciful, just as your Father is merciful.

What were the listeners to do in response to each of those scenarios of abuse and violence? They were to respond with extravagant generosity, expecting nothing in return. Jesus repeated four practical responses: love, do good, bless, and pray. Rather than protecting their possessions, their pride, their reputation, or even their physical safety, Jesus instructed them to respond to the perpetrator with generosity and grace.

Retired Anglican bishop and scholar N.T. Wright says that to understand this teaching of Jesus, we should think of something that we would really like for someone else to do for us—something extravagant, generous, and lavish. Then we should imagine doing that act for the person who has treated us the worst. Difficult though it may be, Wright says that such actions demonstrate the kingdom of God that Jesus preached, a kingdom of "glorious, uproarious, absurd generosity."

Jesus was, however, reminding his followers that this radical generosity being asked of them was the same that God had extended to them. God is merciful, kind to the ungrateful and the wicked (verse 35). God does not love us in order to gain something, but out of extravagant generosity and grace. Following God's example, our love should not be limited to those from whom we can benefit or gain, but be extended beyond our circles of comfort and safety.

Scenic Route

Notice that Jesus' instructions were both spiritual or emotional and practical: love, do good, bless, pray. Praying for your enemies is difficult because it requires acknowledging their humanity and considering them worthy of God's attention. Doing good to your enemy requires an external or public act. It doesn't just require a change of thought, but a willingness to act on that change. It requires concrete expressions of generosity, particularly with regard to our possessions, and it involves a lot of letting go.

When have you been able to respond to maltreatment by doing good, loving, blessing, and praying for the other person? How did the person respond? How do you feel about having done so?

Think of something extravagant, generous, and lavish. Then imagine doing that for the worst person. What is your response to that scenario?

How does God's generosity compare with ours? How have your ideas about generosity changed?

How can you merge Jesus' teachings with the need to stop injustices? Of what instances are you aware when someone offered love in the face of a tremendous injustice?

How do you think God is calling Christians to respond to the violence in our world? How can we be supportive of those who are working for peace?

What material things are part of your "blessed life" that you would be afraid of losing?

We must be very careful in our interpretation of this teaching, especially in relation to those who have suffered violence, abuse, or discrimination. A dangerous and harmful interpretation of this teaching could lead to the silencing of victims and the rewarding of perpetrators. It would be unwise to implement Jesus' teaching as a criminal justice policy.

Accusations of injustice are coming from almost every part of our society, many of them very justified. There is no easy way to reconcile Jesus' teachings with the world as we know it. So, what do we do with this teaching? At what point do we stop letting go of the hurts, the hatred, the injustices, and the abuse?

If everyone gave as Jesus directed, there would be no cries of injustice, hurt, hatred, or abuse. However, we know that the world is imperfect and that such things will continue to happen until God's kingdom comes. As Christians, we are then left to determine how we should react in the face of these injustices. All too often we have looked the other way while someone else was turning the other cheek.

As you think about how Christians are called to respond to these difficult situations, consider this poem attributed to Martin Niemöller:
First they came for the communists, and I did not speak out
  - because I was not a communist;
Then they came for the socialists, and I did not speak out
  - because I was not a socialist;
Then they came for the trade unionists, and I did not speak out
  - because I was not a trade unionist;
Then they came for the Jews, and I did not speak out
  - because I was not a Jew;
Then they came for me
  - and there was no one left to speak out for me.

The responses Jesus called for are not passive, but are bold acts of courage in the face of evil. By following these teachings, we are refusing to allow evil to have power over good, demonstrating that goodness will always prevail.

Of course the only way such a response is possible is if we take seriously the words of Jesus about the blessings and the woes in verses 20-26. If we think that a blessed life is the abundance of possessions, food, and laughter, our response to Jesus' scenarios is to consider ourselves to have been cursed. Generosity from this perspective is difficult, if not impossible, because we are focused on protecting and defending our possessions. We love, do good, bless, and pray for those who don't threaten us, our allies. But to those whom we view as competition, as a threat to what is ours, such actions are not possible.

If we can embrace Jesus' teaching that a blessed life is not measured by material things, we can adopt a different attitude toward both ourselves and others. A godly life is measured by our commitment to loving God and others. It requires a commitment to God over our own desires. The repetition of the words *you* and *your* challenges us to resist the temptation to make ourselves the object and goal of our lives and

84

faith. Verse 36 reminds us of whose kingdom we serve, and instructs us to "be merciful, just as your Father is merciful." If we are to live into this kingdom life, our love, goodness, blessings, and prayers must have no bounds.

Workers Ahead

CAUTION

While walking with a friend, a homeless person approached, asking for money. I always declined to give money in that type of situation, thinking that I was supporting the person's drug or alcohol habit. However, my friend reached into her purse and gave the man a few coins. When I questioned her actions, she simply replied that she was supposed to give. What the person did with the gift was between him and God. My friend's simple act has impacted my thinking about giving ever since.

Read Luke 6:37-38.

"Do not judge, and you will not be judged; do not condemn, and you will not be condemned. Forgive, and you will be forgiven; [38] give, and it will be given to you. A good measure, pressed down, shaken together, running over, will be put into your lap; for the measure you give will be the measure you get back."

Christian doctrine does not embrace the eastern concept of karma. We do not believe in either reincarnation or in salvation by works. Yet, on many occasions, Jesus taught that our actions toward others will determine God's action toward us. We believe that God's love and mercy are not earned, but freely given. However, it is clear that our actions do matter.

"Give and it will be given to you," Jesus said. As we've already seen in Jesus' blessings and woes, what God views as blessing is not likely to match the world's expectations. God's generosity is not necessarily material, but life in its fullness, full of God's love, mercy and grace.

The challenge Jesus placed before the people then, and us today, is, "Are you willing to be as generous to others as you wish God to be to you?"

In what ways might radical generosity be considered a weak response? a courageous response? What fears do you have about not having bounds to your love, goodness, blessings, and prayers?

How does the reward of God's blessing compare with the promise of material blessing?

85

In the Rear View

Bishop Desmond Tutu's response to being knocked to the ground was a demonstration of radical generosity and kindness in the face of evil and wrongdoing. Though his dignity had been bruised and his humanity ignored, he responded with a blessing rather than revenge. Rather than returning evil with evil, he interrupted the cycle by offering generous grace and goodness.

Though our natural inclination is toward self-defense, avoiding those who threaten our blessed life, Jesus calls us in a new direction—to radical openness and generosity. We are called to mirror the character of our merciful God whose love for all of humanity knows no bounds.

It is undoubtedly a difficult teaching, one few of us live up to, and one that should be carefully interpreted. It is a reminder that following Jesus involves letting go of life as we expect and imagine it to embrace God's generous and grace-filled kingdom.

Travel Log

Day 1:

Psalm 67 is a song of thanksgiving for God's generosity to the earth and all its peoples. It includes praise to God for judging with fairness and guiding all nations. Read the psalm aloud if possible, paying particular attention to God's generosity. Reflect on the psalm and make note of any new understandings it brings.

Day 2:

Draw a circle in the space below. Inside the circle write the names of people who are easy for you to love. Outside the circle, write the names of those whom you find it difficult to love—those who have hurt you or those whom you consider to be enemies.

Day 3:

As is healthy and appropriate for you, beside each of the names that you listed outside of your circle in day two, attempt to write one or more of the following: a blessing for that person; a prayer for him or her; a way in which you could do good to that person; a reflection on how you could love that person.

Day 4:

Think of or research a situation in which someone showed radical generosity in the face of evil. Write about that situation and your feelings in regard to it. If you have difficulty thinking of such a situation, consider the response of the Amish community when a gunman entered a one-room school in Pennsylvania, killing five young girls and wounding five others. You can find more about this story by doing an Internet search for "Amish response to school shooting."

Day 5:

Reflect on a time when someone showed you or someone you know radical generosity. What did the person do? What did it take for him or her to show this generosity? What did his or her actions mean to you?

Day 6:

Reflect on a time when you were recently asked to be generous, or had the opportunity to do so. What happened? How did you respond? Why? How do Jesus' words challenge your actions?

Day 7:
Make a list of ways in which you want to commit to a life of radical generosity. Pray that God will give you the faith and courage to follow through with your commitments.

Source
Luke for Everyone, by N.T. Wright. Louisville: Westminster John Knox. 2004.

Opening Doors, Breaking Boundaries

Scripture for lesson: Acts 16:11-15

FAITH LIFE

"In the beginning, December 1986, four congregations committed to shelter homeless people through March 1987. By the end of that winter, 31 congregations had joined. Now we have over 190 congregations in Middle Tennessee and over 6,500 volunteers, in addition to our downtown campus, sheltering almost 1,400 men and women from November 1st through March 31st each season. 365 days a year we offer emergency services, transitional programs, and long-term solutions to help people rebuild their lives" (www.room-intheinn.org/our-story).

This is the story of Room in the Inn (RITI), a ministry of hospitality in Nashville, Tennessee, that began with faith communities that were willing to open their doors to welcome strangers and share their resources. Since its inception, 24 other cities have started RITI programs.

Congregations that participate in RITI's winter shelter program are responsible for hosting 8-15 guests on their assigned nights. It begins with transporting guests from a downtown center to the church, where church members serve dinner. The host churches also provide their guests with a place to sleep, a hot breakfast, a sack lunch for the day ahead, and transportation back to the RITI center.

As a ministry of hospitality, RITI encourages members of the host congregations to spend time in conversation with guests during dinner, to play games and watch movies together afterward. It is this relational element that makes RITI participation such a significant and transformational experience for congregations. Their church building becomes a unique social space where people from vastly differing backgrounds sit around a table while they share food, tell life stories, and play games. It is a space that opens up the possibility of strangers sharing their common humanity, a place for guests and hosts to listen to and respect one another as people with a name and story. As with all good hospitality, it is more than just the provision of physical needs, but the experience of being safe, welcomed, and valued.

When have you been the recipient of good hospitality? When do you/have you shared space with people whose backgrounds are vastly different from your own? What was it like? In what ways does your congregation demonstrate hospitality?

Prep for the Journey

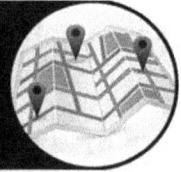

Paul, the man who once committed his life to persecuting Christians, had an encounter with the living Christ after which he became one of the early church's most fervent believers and sharers of the gospel. He seemed compelled to share the good news with those outside of the Jewish tradition, which often resulted in Paul's life being threatened. Some did not agree with Paul and fought against his sharing of the message that Jesus was the Messiah. Despite the leaders in Jerusalem sending him home for his own safety, Paul inevitably was drawn back to the mission field.

Acts 13 and 14 tell us that, called by the Holy Spirit, Paul and Barnabas set sail on their first missionary journey to Cyprus and Asia Minor (modern day Turkey). Whereas the earliest converts to Christianity had been primarily those of the Jewish faith, the gospel was quickly spreading to the Gentile population. When Paul and others began to welcome Gentiles into the communities of faith, a major debate arose between Paul and the other early leaders of the church.

Paul contended that Gentile converts should not be required to be circumcised to become believers. He argued that these new converts were not marked by a physical sign, as in circumcision, but by baptism. The true mark of a convert was a life transformed by the power of the Holy Spirit and the way these converts lived together in community.

Having returned to Jerusalem and convinced the Christian leadership that Gentiles should be welcomed into the Christian fold without forcing them to be circumcised (chapter 15), Paul wanted to make a second journey to encourage and guide these new communities in their life together.

> Who are the "Gentiles" in our society? What would it take to make them feel welcome in our faith communities?

On the Road

While planning his second journey to Cyprus and Asia Minor, Paul experienced a detour in the form of a dream. In Paul's dream, a man in Macedonia was begging him to visit there. Convinced that the Holy Spirit was calling them to go to this man, Paul, Silas, and Timothy headed for Europe and the Roman colony of Philippi.

Read Acts 16:11-15.

We set sail from Troas and took a straight course to Samothrace, the following day to Neapolis, ¹² and from there to Philippi, which is a leading *city of the district of Macedonia and a Roman colony. We remained in this city for some days. ¹³ On the sabbath day we went outside the gate by the river, where we supposed there was a place of prayer; and we sat down and spoke to the women who had gathered there. ¹⁴ A certain woman named Lydia, a worshiper of God, was listening to us; she was from the city of Thyatira and a dealer in purple cloth. The Lord opened her heart to listen eagerly to what was said by Paul. ¹⁵ When she and her household were baptized, she urged us, saying, "If you have judged me to be faithful to the Lord, come and stay at my home." And she prevailed upon us.*

When visiting a new city, Paul usually started his evangelistic ministry by attending the synagogue on the sabbath and addressing the community gathered there. Synagogue worship included a reading of the scripture and a time for interpretation, during which Paul would share his message of good news about Jesus. A visiting teacher was often invited to read and share his interpretation.

In traditional Jewish practice, a male provided the interpretation of scripture to the people, and the presence of 10 males was necessary before the people who had gathered at a synagogue could worship. What Paul found in the pagan city of Philippi was apparently a somewhat unusual and probably insignificant Jewish community. They met outside of the city by the river, and there is no mention of any male worshipers—just a group of women who had gathered to worship God.

Among the group of women whom Paul addressed was a woman named Lydia. Her name was of Greek origin, which suggests she was probably a Gentile. She was from the city of Thyatira in Asia Minor, a city known to have been the center of the textile dying industry. It is there that Lydia would have learned and practiced the specialized trade of producing purple cloth, an expensive and luxury item. It was not unheard of for women to be in a place of social or economic power, but it was certainly unusual. Women usually were dependent on a spouse or male offspring to provide for them economically and to secure their social standing. Lydia however, was a business owner, homeowner, and quite possibly the head of her household.

As someone probably of substantial means, Lydia was unlike most of the women we encounter in scripture, and even many of the men. Yet she had gathered by the river with this group of women to worship God. Whatever Paul's message, it became a holy encounter for Lydia, who responded by being baptized and seeking baptism for her entire household.

Lydia received Paul's message, experienced the transformation of the Holy Spirit, and embraced the good news of Jesus. She and her household received baptism and were welcomed into the life of Christ and the church through the grace and love of God. Now Lydia responds by offering a gift of her own, urging Paul and his companions to come stay at her home.

How are visiting teachers/preachers treated when they are present for worship with your congregation?

What would cause you to invite virtual strangers to stay in your home? What do you think about people who do invite strangers into their lives?

Think about your own response to hearing the good news. How has your response reflected an attitude of giving? of receiving?

Later in chapter 16 (verse 40), after Paul and Silas were released from jail, they returned to Lydia's house, which had apparently become the center for the newly-formed Christian community in Philippi. Lydia's invitation was not just as a place for the travelers to stay, but for believers to gather, worship, and share in one another's lives. She used her resources to provide a space where believers could be a community, and out of which the gospel continued to be made known among the Philippians.

For this woman, the gospel of Jesus was not something just to be received. It was not just something to prop up her social status or reputation. It was a message and way of life that compelled her to respond with generosity, to view her resources as a way in which she could serve and minister to others.

Scenic Route

Paul dreamed about a man urging him to come to Macedonia, but when he arrived he encountered a group of women. We know that Lydia was likely a Gentile worshiper, but given that the region was part of a Roman colony with no prominent synagogue, she was probably not the only Gentile among those who had gathered to worship.

Paul continued his compulsion to share the good news with all who would listen, crossing religious and social boundaries in a radically inclusive ministry. Gentiles were invited into the community of followers of Jesus without having to conform to the Jewish practice of circumcision, and women were invited directly, without the mediation of a male.

Lydia was the recipient of a generous gospel that welcomed her, a Gentile woman, into the community of Christ. Her response of hospitality was equally as radical. In the Roman world, social class was a fixed boundary with little or no movement between the classes. Those classes were hereditary, determined at birth by your family status and honor, with virtually no hope of progressing upwards. The only relationships between the classes would have been that of patronage, of owing your allegiance to someone above you on the social ladder for their provision.

How does your faith call you to cross social and cultural boundaries? How have you acted upon that call?

When Lydia opened her home to Paul and Silas, and then to the new Christian converts, she did so despite the social boundaries of the culture. Rather than operating in her own social class, prioritizing her own status and reputation, she invited strangers from a range of social classes into her home.

Throughout the Gospels, we read Jesus' teachings concerning wealth and the danger of possessions. "How hard it is for those who have wealth to enter the kingdom of God! Indeed, it is easier for a camel to go through the eye of a needle than for someone who is rich to enter the kingdom of God" (Luke 18:24-25). Yet in the actions of Lydia, we see how the wealthy have the potential to use their wealth for the good of God's kingdom.

The encounter of Paul and Lydia demonstrates both the radical generosity of the gospel and the life to which we are called in response. A wealthy, Gentile woman was invited and initiated into the Christian community, and she responded with boundary-breaking hospitality. The normal social divisions of male and female, Jew and Gentile, rich and poor did not apply for Christ or his Church.

Workers Ahead

One of the essentials for a community is a shared space. For the early Christians, this space was a home, like Lydia's. For most of us, this space is our church building on a Sunday morning. However, Lydia's story should raise some questions for us: How are we using our space? For whom are we using our space?

Our churches need to be spaces where community groups, support groups, or ministries to strangers can be held. Sometimes, people don't feel comfortable in an actual church building, so we may need to create space for church to happen in a coffee shop, bar, restaurant, bowling alley, or some other location, making sure that newcomers are always welcomed.

Beyond our church buildings, this story also raises the question about how we use our personal resources to provide hospitality for others. Like Lydia, it may mean we are to think of our homes as places where others are welcome.

In recent years, we have seen the emergence of digital spaces in which communities have formed. Facebook groups, blogs, and websites connect people across the globe around particular interests or concerns, facilitating a new kind of relationship and community that does not require a physical space, but needs a host to create them. The church can offer digital hospitality by starting a blog or forum that provides space for people to connect and support one another.

Churches should be places of hospitality that welcome diversity, invite persons from a range of social groups and backgrounds, and provide a refuge from a divided society. God has generously welcomed us into the divine community of grace and love, and we are called to welcome others in the same way.

Think of people who have used their wealth for the good of God's kingdom. How have those people affected your willingness to give of your own resources? How might your actions encourage others to give?

When have you experienced hospitality that crossed normal social divisions? What things divide us now? How does the church challenge or reinforce those divisions?

How can we provide a space to welcome and connect with others in our homes, workplaces, and communities? How might the gospel that has welcomed you into the community of Christ be calling you to create space that invites others into that community?

In the Rear View

We began with the story of four churches that opened their doors to strangers whose backgrounds were very different from their own. The buildings that provided a space for their Christian community to worship became a space where men and women without homes could spend the night. It became a space where they could sit around tables together, creating a new kind of community.

The gospel calls upon us to create new communities in the ways that Jesus demonstrated—breaking down barriers and treating all people as brothers and sisters, as children of God. As we have received generously from God, we are called to respond generously. As we have been welcomed into this community, we are called to welcome others.

Day 1:

Psalm 31 is a prayer of trust in God, but also a prayer for help. The psalmist acknowledges the need to feel safe and protected and describes God as a refuge, rock, fortress, and a shelter in a time of distress and attack. As you read the psalm, imagine it from the perspective of someone other than yourself. Reflect on the importance of a safe space. Record some of your thoughts below.

Day 2:

Make a list of the ways in which you have received hospitality from the church, Christians, or from Christ. How have you been welcomed and been able to experience a place of safety?

Day 3:

Read Paul's words in Galatians 3:23-29. How do they relate to the Lydia-Paul encounter in Acts 16? What do they tell us about the Church of Jesus?

Day 4:

In the space below, draw a shape that represents your church, then draw a large circle around that shape, leaving some empty space. Inside the church shape, write the names of some of the civic and social groups that are represented in your congregation. Then inside the circle but outside of the church shape, write the names of some groups that are in your community but are not represented in your congregation. Consider why those groups are not represented among the members of your congregation.

Day 5:

Make a list of words that describe what a hospitable community would look or feel like. Consider how you can encourage the communities in which you participate to become more hospitable.

Day 6:

Create a list of ways in which you could use your home, church, social media account, etc. as a place to create a hospitable community. Be imaginative and creative!

Day 7:

   Lydia's response of generosity came from the transformation of the Holy Spirit that "opened her heart" to the message. Write a prayer asking God's Holy Spirit to transform your thinking and desires to enable you to give generously.

Giving Up the Rat Race

Scripture for lesson: Philippians 1:12-18; 2:1-18

L
FAITH
F
E

"Once upon a time, a tiny striped caterpillar burst from the egg which had been home for so long." Stripe is a caterpillar in Trina Paulus' allegory *Hope for the Flowers*. After eating leaf after leaf, Stripe thought to himself, *There must be more to life than just eating and getting bigger... it's getting dull*. Stripe left the tree of his childhood in search of something more. Having had little success, Stripe came across a column that stretched high up into the clouds. The column was completely made up of caterpillars like him. "Maybe I'll find what I'm looking for here," he said.

Curious, Stripe asks another crawler what's at the top. "I don't know," was the response, "but it must be awfully good because everyone is rushing there." Watching as crawler after crawler plunged into the fray, Stripe sensed that not a second more could be wasted, so he followed suit. Pushed, kicked, and stepped on, Stripe quickly realized that he must "climb or be climbed."

Finally Stripe made it to the top, only to realize nothing was there. Looking around, he saw that his pillar was just one of thousands, full of millions of caterpillars climbing to the top of nowhere. Just then, Stripe saw his friend Yellow. She had decided not to climb, choosing instead to go into a tiny dark space, a world quite opposite the tower. Through patience and by enduring a death of sorts, she emerged from the cocoon, transformed. At the sight of Yellow, Stripe realized that climbing the tower was futile, for butterflies alone can reach the sky.

Stripe began to descend the pillar, whispering to the other caterpillars, "I've been to the top and nothing is there... we can become butterflies... we can fly." Most ignored him while some responded with ridicule, saying, "He's just bitter. I bet he's never even been to the top." Others responded with anguish, "Don't say it, even if it's true. What else can we do?"

What does this story say to you? How does Paulus' allegory challenge or speak to our world? In the climb of the pillar, how were others viewed? How do we treat others?

Prep for the Journey

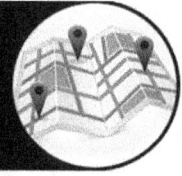

Philippi was a city in what was eastern Macedonia, now modern-day Greece, which has been abandoned since the fourteenth century. In the first century, it was a Roman colony on the Via Egnatia, a main road that provided easier access to Rome from the outlying areas. It is likely because of this road that Paul ended up in Philippi on his second missionary journey.

As a result of Paul sharing the gospel with the people of Philippi, a community of believers formed, likely gathering to worship in individual's homes. Paul remained in communication with these house churches through colleagues who traveled through the area and by letter.

The Book of Philippians is a letter from Paul to the church in Philippi. Like the letters of modern day, it shared personal messages and discussed a variety of topics. This letter would have been read aloud when the people gathered for worship. Neither they nor Paul would have imagined that letters would eventually be intended only for an individual and considered private!

We know that Paul wrote this letter from prison, but we are not certain of its location. In comparing Philippians with letters to the Galatians and the Corinthians, we can easily see that Paul has a deeply personal relationship with the Philippians. As indicated by the letter, he did not experience the same kind of conflict and problems with them as he did with the other two communities. However, his concern with the unity of the church in Philippi does seem to reflect that he perceived there was some kind of threat at hand.

What method of personal communication do you prefer? How do you feel when you receive a personal letter?

On the Road

Paul is well known for having spoken his mind, often in ways that chastised the believers, but he also gave encouragement. He knew that the believers' lives would become increasingly difficult, and he wanted them to have the gift of being able to stand firm in their beliefs about Christ. By standing firm, they would give encouragement to others.

Read Philippians 2:1-4.

If then there is any encouragement in Christ, any consolation from love, any sharing in the Spirit, any compassion and sympathy, ² make my joy complete: be of the same mind, having the same love, being in

Who encourages you? How do you encourage others? What form does that encouragement take?

full accord and of one mind. ³ Do nothing from selfish ambition or conceit, but in humility regard others as better than yourselves. ⁴ Let each of you look not to your own interests, but to the interests of others.

Remembering that this letter was meant for public reading in a house church, it is helpful to understand that Paul's references to "you" were directed to each individual listener as well as to the whole group of believers. We can only properly understand his instruction to be "of one mind" if we imagine it being read to a group of people. As people who have heard the good news of Jesus and who shared with him in new life through the Holy Spirit, Paul called them to unity of heart and mind.

In our contemporary world with the benefit of modern psychology, we may interpret Paul's call to humility as addressing our self-image and identity, which is a very internal kind of humility. This type of humility is a way of thinking about ourselves and our worth in relation to others. It is difficult for us, however, to keep in mind that the first-century Mediterranean culture was a world without modern psychology or self-awareness. That world was very much an external one wherein a person's value was seen primarily as the ways in which he or she interacted with the society. Paul's call to humility is more than just a way of thinking; it's a way of behaving in relationship to others.

Biblical writers make it clear that true faith always has implications for the way we live, often ones that require a radical change and that don't fit with the cultural values or expectations. A faith that is primarily internal doesn't require us to give much, but Paul called for a community that would be shaped by self-giving and self-sacrifice. This attitude was quite the opposite of the Philippian culture, which was inherently elitist. Instead of attempting to climb the ladder and improve their own place in the world, Paul called the believers to reject the Roman value system and live with a regard for others.

Read Philippians 2:5-11.
Let the same mind be in you that was in Christ Jesus,

⁶ who, though he was in the form of God,
did not regard equality with God
as something to be exploited,
⁷ but emptied himself,
taking the form of a slave,
being born in human likeness.
And being found in human form,
⁸ he humbled himself
and became obedient to the point of death—
even death on a cross.

⁹ Therefore God also highly exalted him
and gave him the name
that is above every name,

What are the differences between thinking humbly and living humbly? What might we risk by living humbly?

How would you describe the culture of the United States today? What might Paul say to us? What does it mean to live with a regard for others?

How do your ideas of power and success compare to Paul's ideas? the Roman culture's? How might Jesus' example be both freeing and a burden? What might be the impact of this kind of living for the Church?

¹⁰ so that at the name of Jesus
every knee should bend,
in heaven and on earth and under the earth,
¹¹ and every tongue should confess
that Jesus Christ is Lord,
to the glory of God the Father.

In verses 6-11 Paul quoted what is widely thought to have been a hymn. Its origin and content is disputed, but there is little doubt what he intended to communicate to the Philippians. Their Savior voluntarily lowered and emptied himself, so they should be of the same mind.

Refusing to participate in one's cultural value system is not easy. That kind of life ends in death. At worst, it is a physical death; at best, it is a social one. Either way, most of us realize that living with a concern for others doesn't advance us very far up the ladder of success or status. Many people would declare that such concern is naive or outright foolish.

The hymn, however, offers an alternative conclusion, a reversal of the social expectation. While Jesus' humility and self-emptying should have ended in his humiliation, they ultimately resulted in his glory. All of creation declared that Jesus is Lord.

In the Roman Empire, Caesar was Lord. Caesar was on top of the social status pile to which every knee bowed. He achieved glory through his power, which was upheld by an entire society. This hymn reveals that what looked to be true in the present, would ultimately be just a fantasy. True power and glory are not found in selfish ambition, coercion, or competition, but in voluntary humility and self-sacrifice.

"Don't be fooled," Paul was saying to the Philippians. They were not to live according to the cultural models of glory, but by the gospel. They were not to live according to the patterns of Caesar, but of Jesus. Such a life is primarily concerned about others rather than self. It means living in accordance with the call of God rather than our own ambition, and it requires giving up the chase for the things that do not satisfy.

Scenic Route

When reading this passage, we need to keep in mind the situation from which Paul wrote. We turn to chapter one for a glimpse:

Read Philippians 1:12-18.
I want you to know, beloved, that what has happened to me has actually helped to spread the gospel, ¹³ so that it has become known

throughout the whole imperial guard and to everyone else that my imprisonment is for Christ; 14 and most of the brothers and sisters, having been made confident in the Lord by my imprisonment, dare to speak the word with greater boldness and without fear.

15 Some proclaim Christ from envy and rivalry, but others from goodwill. 16 These proclaim Christ out of love, knowing that I have been put here for the defense of the gospel; 17 the others proclaim Christ out of selfish ambition, not sincerely but intending to increase my suffering in my imprisonment. 18 What does it matter? Just this, that Christ is proclaimed in every way, whether out of false motives or true; and in that I rejoice.

Yes, and I will continue to rejoice.

Paul had a promising future ahead of him before his encounter with Jesus, including excellent social status, a strong reputation, and religious power. Following the call of Jesus led him to turn his back on his religious standing and his Roman citizenship, which ultimately led to his arrest.

As the example of Jesus so clearly demonstrates, the gospel life is one that was not easily accepted by either the secular or religious realm. Paul was very explicit with the Philippians about the challenges that they faced and the fear that would accompany them, yet he also expressed the possibility of joy amidst it all.

At times Paul seemed a little too eager for people to experience conflict and suffering. It is important to remember that Paul wrote to specific churches where imprisonment and suffering were very real possibilities in the first century. These circumstances are not likely to be realities for twenty-first century Christians who live in the United States. Choosing the story that will guide our lives is, however, a reality for all of us. Paul called the believers to live in ways that showed their commitment to the gospel rather than success or citizenship.

With a commitment to the gospel message in mind, we see that part of Paul's emphasis on unity was because he saw it as essential for living in a world where the believers would face many challenges to their faith. Faith is not a task to be accomplished by the individual believer, but by the community of believers living and worshiping as one mind and with one purpose.

Workers Ahead

The Letter to the Philippians offers us an opportunity to reflect on our Christian congregations and communities, asking how they compare when contrasted to Paul's ideals. Are they places where group members share in unity of mind and heart, acting with more regard

How did your life change when you encountered Christ?

How does Christianity clash with our culture? In what instances do you think it should clash more? What are some of the positive experiences of your Christian community? negative experiences?

for others than themselves? How do the attitudes of the congregation reflect a commitment to the values of the gospel of Jesus? to the culture? How willing are members to embrace the call to be self-giving in the face of the challenges and risks?

Likewise it offers a challenge to the individual, revealing that faith is not just a matter of belief, but a matter of action and a call to pattern our lives after Jesus. It warns against any ideas that faith results in prosperity and an easy life, or that it can be lived out alone.

In the Rear View

Paul's message is not too dissimilar from that of Stripe descending the pillar, whispering, "There's nothing up there" to the millions of caterpillars climbing to the top of nowhere. Paul reversed the way the Philippians thought about the world, telling them that true glory is found not by climbing all over one another as if in competition, but by giving up the rat race and considering others as more important than ourselves.

How would you describe your congregation or faith community in light of Paul's ideals? How are you connected to and invested in your community of faith? In what other ways do you need to become invested?

How do you live out Paul's message? In what ways do you need to "give up the rat race"?

Travel Log

Day 1:

Psalm 10 begins as a prayer of lament as the psalmist observes those who take advantage of the poor and vulnerable. Their actions are indicative of people who are trying to climb the ladder of self-glory at the expense of others. Read the passage aloud. Try to write verses or phrases of the psalm in your own words.

Day 2:

Draw a ladder in the blank space. What ladder are you tempted or encouraged to climb that you know is ultimately unfulfilling or even destructive? What steps would be necessary for you to climb it? How do those steps reflect your faith?

Day 3:

How would you describe your community of faith? What words come to mind when you think of its members? In what ways do they reflect Paul's ideals of unity, humility, and self-sacrifice?

Day 4:

Make two columns. In one column write words that you think describe the characteristics of a healthy Christian community. In the other, write words that you think describe characteristics of an unhealthy Christian community. Consider which ones apply to your faith community, if any. How can you be an instrument of any needed change?

Day 5:

From the list you made yesterday, choose some characteristics that indicate the need for personal improvement. Write a reflection and/or prayer in response.

Day 6:

Make a list of concrete, practical ways that you can give of yourself to others today. Opportunities are plentiful when you open yourself to them.

Day 7:

Re-read and meditate on the hymn of Paul referenced in Philippians 2:6-11. After reading it several times, write a prayer of commitment to living in the way of Jesus rather than the way of success and glory.

Grace: From Recipients to Participants

Scripture for lesson: 1 Corinthians 16:1-4; 2 Corinthians 8:1-15, 24

Each summer over 200 Cumberland Presbyterian youth and adults gather to worship, play, and learn as they become community during the Cumberland Presbyterian Youth Conference (CPYC). A week or two later, another 200 Cumberland Presbyterians gather for the day-long celebration of Children's Fest, which also provides a time for participants to worship, play, learn, and form community.

As a small denomination, remaining connected is important to Cumberland Presbyterians. Many lifelong friendships begin at these events. They foster a sense of community across a wide geographical area, weaving together our shared story, commitments, and purpose as a church.

The denomination also hosts a minister's conference and a leadership development conference (The Forum), produces resources for Christian discipleship, distributes the *Missionary Messenger* and *The Cumberland Presbyterian* magazines, and oversees the work of its missionaries. They educate and train people for vocation and ministry at Bethel University and Memphis Theological Seminary. Then there's the Children's Home in Denton, Texas, that cares for at-risk children and families, and the General Assembly that oversees the denomination as a whole, including theological, social, and legal issues.

A denomination enables Christians from across the globe who share convictions, beliefs, and mission to operate as a united body, combining efforts, resources, and ministries to serve its congregations and minister to the world. It is a large and complex system, and none of it is done for profit. Congregations and denominations are fueled by the energy of the people and the resources that they share.

In the Cumberland Presbyterian Church, congregations are asked to give a tithe of their income to Our United Outreach (OUO) as a means of supporting the work of the denomination. The committee that oversees OUO sets giving targets that are approximately half the amount that could be expected if each congregation gave its tithe, yet the denomination has failed to meet its goals for several consecutive years. As its resources dwindle, the denomination is faced with some difficult questions—not only about what work it will continue do, but about the unity and commitment of its congregations.

What does it mean to you to be part of the Cumberland Presbyterian denomination? From what denominational resources or programs do you benefit?

Prep for the Journey

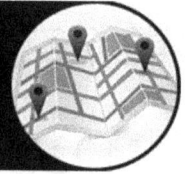

The Book of Acts provides an account of Paul's missionary journeys and the establishment of Christian communities from Jerusalem to Rome. As he was unable to remain with the churches, Paul wrote letters to address their issues and concerns, encourage them in the faith, and remind them of their responsibilities. Paul's letters give us an insight into his relationship with these churches, the issues that they were facing, and his words of guidance to them.

When the leaders of the church in Jerusalem commissioned Barnabas and Paul to minister to the Gentiles throughout the Mediterranean, they asked only one thing: Remember the poor, a reference to believers in Jerusalem who were struggling to survive. Jesus' followers in Jerusalem would have been treated as outcasts, limiting their opportunities for work. Many of the early believers fled Jerusalem to avoid this type of persecution.

How are believers being persecuted today? How can you offer encouragement to those who are in such situations?

On the Road

Believing that the Gentiles needed to help their Christian brothers and sisters in Jerusalem, Paul included this need in the letters he wrote to the churches in Galatia, Rome, and Corinth. After all, the Gentiles would not have come to know Jesus as Messiah without the faithful witness of the believers in Jerusalem.

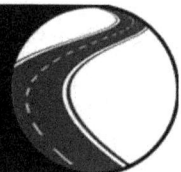

How do you feel about helping other faith communities? Why?

Read 1 Corinthians 16:1-4.

Now concerning the collection for the saints: you should follow the directions I gave to the churches of Galatia. ² On the first day of every week, each of you is to put aside and save whatever extra you earn, so that collections need not be taken when I come. ³ And when I arrive, I will send any whom you approve with letters to take your gift to Jerusalem. ⁴ If it seems advisable that I should go also, they will accompany me.

The Corinthians had apparently already been told about the collection and seem to have asked Paul about it in a previous letter. Paul responded by telling them to set aside additional funds on the first day of each week. We don't know the meaning of "whatever extra you earn"; we simply know that Paul wanted the Corinthians to set it aside as an offering for Jerusalem's poor.

The short instruction in Paul's first letter to the Corinthians suggests that he sensed little or no opposition to his initial request.

How do you set aside funds for special needs? What restrictions do you place on how you use those funds?

However, by the time he wrote the second letter, it is clear that things had not gone as he had expected.

Read 2 Corinthians 8:1-15.

We want you to know, brothers and sisters, about the grace of God that has been granted to the churches of Macedonia; [2] for during a severe ordeal of affliction, their abundant joy and their extreme poverty have overflowed in a wealth of generosity on their part. [3] For, as I can testify, they voluntarily gave according to their means, and even beyond their means, [4] begging us earnestly for the privilege of sharing in this ministry to the saints— [5] and this, not merely as we expected; they gave themselves first to the Lord and, by the will of God, to us, [6] so that we might urge Titus that, as he had already made a beginning, so he should also complete this generous undertaking among you. [7] Now as you excel in everything—in faith, in speech, in knowledge, in utmost eagerness, and in our love for you—so we want you to excel also in this generous undertaking.

[8] I do not say this as a command, but I am testing the genuineness of your love against the earnestness of others. [9] For you know the generous act of our Lord Jesus Christ, that though he was rich, yet for your sakes he became poor, so that by his poverty you might become rich. [10] And in this matter I am giving my advice: it is appropriate for you who began last year not only to do something but even to desire to do something— [11] now finish doing it, so that your eagerness may be matched by completing it according to your means. [12] For if the eagerness is there, the gift is acceptable according to what one has—not according to what one does not have. [13] I do not mean that there should be relief for others and pressure on you, but it is a question of a fair balance between [14] your present abundance and their need, so that their abundance may be for your need, in order that there may be a fair balance. [15] As it is written,

"The one who had much did not have too much,
and the one who had little did not have too little."

Verse 10 seems to suggest that the Corinthians were struggling to finish the project that they had begun the previous year. Although Paul stopped short of demanding they complete the offering, his feelings were clear. First he used the Macedonian churches of Philippi and Thessalonica as an example of generous and gracious giving. Despite both of these churches having experienced a "severe ordeal of affliction" that had caused poverty, they continued to give abundantly, joyfully, and sacrificially. These churches were not forced to give, nor did they have to be encouraged; they simply longed to be involved in the ministry to the poor of Jerusalem, apparently without regard to their own sacrifice or scarcity.

Paul pointed out the example of the generosity of Jesus, reminding them that the grace they received through Jesus came through great humility and sacrifice. His use of Jesus as an example highlighted the hypocrisy of their unwillingness to act likewise to their brothers and sisters in Jerusalem.

How do you react when another group is held up as an example? Why do you think that those who have little are usually so willing to share with others?

Why do you think the churches of Macedonia were able to give generously while the Corinthians were reluctant to do so? What reasons do some churches list for their struggle to give? How giving is your congregation—both materially and in grace?

How might an emphasis on grace transform attitudes toward giving? If responding to the needs of others is a test of love, how might you and your congregation measure?

It is not that Paul wanted the Corinthians to suffer scarcity, but he wanted the resources of God's people to be balanced. While their brothers and sisters were suffering, Paul wanted them to see their abundance as an opportunity to share grace. Finally he made an appeal from scripture, referencing Exodus 16:18 and God's provision of manna and quail to the Israelites in the wilderness. God's ideal is the provision for all, and the Corinthians had an opportunity, if not an obligation, to participate in that vision.

Scenic Route

In 2 Corinthians 8, the Greek word for grace is used six times. It has been translated as a privilege, a generous undertaking, and a generous act. Though these translations may be helpful in interpreting the text, they lose the emphasis that is achieved through the repetition. Paul's instruction was grounded in grace. It was through God's grace that the churches in Macedonia were able to give so generously. Those churches longed to be able to make an offering because they viewed it as an opportunity to pass on that grace to their brothers and sisters who were in need. Paul and Titus continued that act of grace among the Corinthians, urging them to demonstrate their excellence as a faithful community by excelling in grace.

Grace, grace, and more grace. Christian communities respond with generosity because they are the recipients of God's grace in Jesus Christ. They recognize that God has acted in the person of Jesus to bring salvation to them, to restore them into the beloved community. They recognize that all things are a gift of God—not ours to hoard, but to share. Convinced by their trust in God the Creator, and the saving acts of Jesus their Redeemer, Christian people respond in the power of the Holy Spirit to live lives full of the grace that they have received in abundance.

For Paul, grace was not just something to be received. It was something that filled one so completely that it overflowed and had to be offered to another. We sense that the Corinthians had received God's grace, but they were reluctant to share in it. They may have forgotten God's grace to them, lost sight of the life of Jesus, or feared making themselves vulnerable by sharing their resources with others. Paul did not pretend that sharing in grace was easy; he was explicit about the struggle and suffering of the Macedonian churches and about the suffering of Jesus. This challenging request would test the commitment of their love.

Although relieving the need of the poor in Jerusalem was a primary concern, Paul was also concerned with the bigger picture. At the heart of his vision for the church was unity between the believers—unity that refused the divisions of male or female, Jew or Gentile, rich or poor. In the Church of Jesus, believers are equals, united in common love and care for one another.

It was this grand vision that enabled the Gentiles to enter the community, proclaiming that they were no less than their Jewish believing brothers and sisters. It was this vision that enabled the Corinthians to have full access to and membership in the body of believers. This same vision challenged their response to the believers in Jerusalem who needed assistance.

Paul had talked about unity in Christ, but would the church he had started in Corinth demonstrate to the skeptics in Jerusalem that they truly shared in the common faith in Jesus? Or would their reluctance to share in the pain of their brothers and sisters result in a family fallout, destroying the project before it got started?

Workers Ahead

Read 2 Corinthians 8:24.

Therefore openly before the churches, show them the proof of your love and of our reason for boasting about you.

Much of contemporary religious language treats grace solely as something that is received from God. The priority is on receiving grace, primarily that which saves. The flagship phrase of the Protestant Reformation was "faith by grace alone," emphasizing that we cannot save ourselves and are reliant on God's action to renew and restore us.

With such a heavy emphasis on receiving grace, we should be more inclined to respond with grateful and generous hearts to others. Perhaps we have been so consumed with possessing God's grace that we have neglected to pay attention to our participation in it.

Participating in God's grace does not only mean telling others about it and inviting them to receive it, but being living and breathing expressions of it. It means living with a love that's as radical and generous as that which we received from God through Jesus. Paul did not dictate whom we should choose to support, how, or when, but it's clear that charity and generosity are key aspects of living faithfully as people of grace.

Where do you detect a lack of unity within the Christian community? How might grace create or restore unity?

How does your congregation act as part of a larger body of believers? How does your response to giving reflect your relationship to the larger community or denomination?

When have you experienced grace through the charity or generosity of someone else? How might you be a living and breathing expression of God's free grace to others? How might our failure to live as people of grace be viewed as hypocrisy?

In the Rear View

What dreams do you have for your church's ministries? How can you move those dreams toward becoming a reality?

Like Paul, many of our denominations and congregations have dreams of what their ministries could look like, for how they could show signs of God's grace in the world. They dream of forming people into communities that are dedicated to the ways of God's kingdom, but those dreams require the people's commitment and their resources. We are the body of Christ—the hands and feet that can be the concrete signs and expressions of God's saving grace, but only if we are willing to act. Only when God's kingdom becomes the top priority in our lives will we be the Church of which Paul dreamed. Only when our vision is colored by the life, death, and resurrection of Jesus can we be who God has called us to be, giving generously of the grace that has been given to us. Only then will we be able to fulfill our calling as the Church.

Travel Log

Day 1:

Psalm 66 is a call to worship. The psalmist remembered and proclaimed how God liberated the people from slavery and oppression, sustaining them through suffering. The psalmist's response to God's grace and generosity was to offer worship in word and action. Reflect on why you worship God. Record some of your thoughts below.

Day 2:

Re-read Paul's words about the example of Jesus in 2 Corinthians 8:9. Write some thoughts as to how the example of Jesus challenges or encourages you.

Day 3:

In the space below, write a few sentences or make a list of words that indicate what your denomination means to you. If you don't know much about it, make a list of questions to ask your pastor or someone who has been a member for a long time.

Day 4:

In the space below, write the words the Church exists to.... Complete the sentence with as many different answers as possible.

Day 5:

Re-write Paul's words about the Macedonian churches (2 Corinthians 8:3-5) in the space below. How do these words challenge or encourage you in your attitude about giving?

Day 6:

Make a list of the ways that you currently share your resources with your congregation and/or denomination. Include your time, energy, finances, acts of service, and creativity. Note the ways in which you could increase your contributions.

Day 7:

As you reflect upon your exploration of the theme of giving, complete the following three sentences with some conclusions that you will take away:

1) "In a world that is…"

2) "There is a God who…"

3) "So I will…"